THE CAT COMPENDIUM

the cat compendium

EDITED BY

Ann Currah

WILLIAM KIMBER · LONDON

First published in Great Britain in 1972 by
WILLIAM KIMBER AND CO. LIMITED
Godolphin House, 22a Queen Anne's Gate,
London SW1H 9AE

SBN 7183 0222 2

Printed in Great Britain by
Redwood Press Limited, Trowbridge, Wiltshire

Acknowledgments

For permission to reprint the copyrighted material in this compendium, the editor gratefully acknowledges the following:

"The Ad-Dressing of Cats" from *Old Possum's Book of Practical Cats*, by T. S. Eliot. Reprinted by permission of Faber and Faber Ltd.

"Arthur the Teevee Cat" by Angela Milne. Reprinted by permission of *Punch.*

"Basta, A Holy Cat of Bubastis" from *Laura Was My Camel* by Arthur Weigall. Published by Butterworth & Co. Ltd. and reprinted by permission of John Farquharson Ltd.

Extract from *The Cat Horoscope Book*, written and illustrated by Liz Tresilian, copyright 1967 by Liz Tresilian; published by permission of Arlington Books.

"The Cat and the Moon" by William Butler Yeats from *The Collected Poems of W. B. Yeats*; reprinted with permission of Mr M. B. Yeats and MacMillan & Co. (London).

"The Cat That Walked by Himself" from *Just So Stories* by Rudyard Kipling; reprinted by permission of Mrs George Bambridge and MacMillan & Co. (London).

Extract from *ESP* by Susy Smith, copyright 1962 by Pyramid Publications, Inc. Reprinted by permission of Pyramid Publications.

"Feelings," copyright 1926 by Harcourt, Brace & Jovanovich Inc.; copyright 1954 by Melville Cane. Reprinted from *So That It Flower* by Melville Cane by permission of Harcourt, Brace & Jovanovich Inc.

"How Cats Came to Purr" by John Bennett, from the *Pigtail of Ah Lee Ben Loo*, reprinted by permission of John H. Bennett, Executor for the estate of John Bennett.

"Kitten's Escapade" reproduced from *The Times* by permission.

Excerpt from *Mr Cat* by George Freedly. Published by The Souvenir Press Ltd. and reprinted by permission.

"New Conquest of the Matterhorn" from the *Alpine Journal*, reprinted by permission of T. S. Blakeney.

Extract from "Up Country" reprinted by permission of Thurlow Craig and the *Sunday Express*.

"Why Cat is Indoors and Dog Outside in Cold" from *Folktales of Ireland*, edited and translated by Sean O'Sullivan, copyright 1966 by The University of Chicago Press.

The editor also wishes to thank the Babylon Translation Service for its translation of the excerpt from Chapter I of E. T. A. Hoffmann's *Lebensansichten Des Katers Murr*.

Every effort has been made to get in touch with owners of copyrighted material, but the editor would be grateful if any inadvertent omissions were brought to her attention.

Chapter opening illustrations:

Page 3, German woodcut, c. 1500, Courtesy the Cooper Union Museum.

Page 16, Egyptian Goddess Bast, from *Moncrif's Cats* by F. A. P. De Mincrif.

Page 39, From "Cat's Dream," by Utamaro, Courtesy New York Public Library.

Page 53, "Foss Passant," drawing by Edward Lear, Courtesy New York Public Library.

Page 83, Cheshire Cat from *Alice in Wonderland,* by Lewis Carroll, drawing by Sir John Tenniel.

To Sampson and to Jenny and in memory of Timothy, a battle-scarred warrior, who was certainly the twentieth-century reincarnation of *The Cat That Walked by Himself*.

CONTENTS

To Someone very Good and Just,
Who has proved worthy of her trust,
A Cat will sometimes condescend—
The Dog is everybody's friend.

Oliver Hereford

If man could be crossed with the cat,
it would improve man but deteriorate the cat.

Mark Twain

EDITOR'S INTRODUCTION

Pasht, Pyewacket, Puss, and Puddy Tat are just a few of the many names that have been given to cats. The human fascination with, and fear of, and friendship for *Felis catus,* the domestic cat, must have begun as long ago as prehistoric times.

Rudyard Kipling, in a story called *The Cat That Walked by Himself,* gives a delightful explanation of how the cat first may have decided to join early man (or rather, woman) in his cave. Cat made a shrewd bargain which allowed him to keep his independence and yet join the domestic circle. In exchange for warmth from the fire and a bowl of milk, Cat agreed to play with the baby and to chase mice. He would, of course, have chased mice naturally. Woman agreed to the bargain, and puss became a familiar part of history, and one of man's most popular pets.

The cult of the cat has existed for thousands of years. Over two thousand years before Christ, Egyptians in the Nile River valley worshiped cats. Intricately wrapped mummy remains of these early cats have been discovered in Egypt. In America and England today, people who are cat lovers and admirers are said to belong to "the cat fancy." All through man's history, stories, superstitions, and anecdotes about cats —some fact and some fiction—have been remembered and often recorded. Cat proverbs as well as familiar cat sayings are known to us all.

What is it about cats that led a whole nation to worship the animal as a god, that inspired terror in the hearts of men and women of medieval times, that inspired hundreds of anonymous and famous writers to describe and attempt to understand the creature, and that has driven modern man to accord the cat respect and affection which often borders on the worshipful attitude of ancient Egyptians? The answers, of course, range from the frivolous—"cats are fuzzy, furry, lovable pets"— to the sublime— "cats seem to be the most intelligent of animals."

Here is a selection of some of the things men have felt and written about cats. *The Cat Compendium* makes no boast of being a complete record of cat information or of cat writings —it is only a sampling of the editor's favorite pieces about the cat, compiled here in anticipation that readers will enjoy the selections and become firm converts to the "cat fancy."

THE CAT COMPENDIUM

THE CAT THAT WALKED BY HIMSELF

by Rudyard Kipling, from *Just So Stories*

Hear and attend and listen; for this befell and behappened and became and was, O my Best Beloved, when the Tame animals were wild. The Dog was wild, and the Horse was wild, and the Pig was wild—as wild as wild could be—and they walked in the Wet Wild Woods by their wild lones. But the wildest of all the wild animals was the Cat. He walked by himself, and all places were alike to him.

Of course the Man was wild too. He was dreadfully wild. He didn't even begin to be tame till he met the Woman, and she told him that she did not like living in his wild ways. She picked out a nice dry Cave, instead of a heap of wet leaves, to lie down in; and she strewed clean sand on the floor; and she lit a nice fire of wood at the back of the Cave; and she hung a dried wild-horse skin, tail-down, across the opening of the Cave; and she said, "Wipe your fect, dear, when you come in, and now we'll keep house."

That night, Best Beloved, they ate wild sheep roasted on the hot stones, and flavoured with wild garlic and wild pepper; and wild duck stuffed with wild rice and wild fenugreek and wild coriander; and marrow-bones of wild oxen; and wild cherries, and wild grenadillas. Then the Man went to sleep in front of the fire ever so happy; but the Woman sat up, combing her hair. She took the bone of the shoulder of mutton—the big fat blade-bone—and she looked at the wonderful marks on it, and she threw more wood on the fire, and she made a Magic. She made the First Singing Magic in the world.

Out in the Wet Wild Woods all the wild animals gathered together where they could see the light of the fire a long way off, and they wondered what it meant.

Then Wild Horse stamped with his wild foot and said, "O my Friends and O my Enemies, why have the Man and the Woman made that great light in that great Cave, and what harm will it do us?"

Wild Dog lifted up his wild nose and smelled the smell of roast mutton, and said, "I will go up and see and look, and say; for I think it is good. Cat, come with me."

"Nenni!" said the Cat. "I am the Cat who walks by himself, and all places are alike to me. I will not come."

"Then we can never be friends again," said Wild Dog, and he trotted off to the Cave. But when he had gone a little way the Cat said to himself, "All places are alike to me. Why should I not go too and see and look and come away at my own liking." So he slipped after Wild Dog softly, very softly, and hid himself where he could hear everything.

When Wild Dog reached the mouth of the Cave he lifted up the dried horse-skin with his nose and sniffed the beautiful smell of the roast mutton, and the Woman, looking at the blade-bone, heard him, and laughed, and said, "Here comes the first. Wild Thing out of the Wild Woods, what do you want?"

Wild Dog said, "O my Enemy and Wife of my Enemy, what is this that smells so good in the Wild Woods?"

Then the Woman picked up a roasted mutton-bone and threw it to Wild Dog, and said, "Wild Thing out of the Wild Woods, taste and try." Wild Dog gnawed the bone, and it was more delicious than anything he had ever tasted, and he said, "O my Enemy and Wife of my Enemy, give me another."

The Woman said, "Wild Thing out of the Wild Woods, help my Man to hunt through the day and guard this Cave at night, and I will give you as many roast bones as you need."

"Ah!" said the Cat, listening. "This is a very wise Woman, but she is not so wise as I am."

Wild Dog crawled into the Cave and laid his head on the Woman's lap, and said, "O my Friend and Wife of my Friend, I will help your Man to hunt through the day, and at night I will guard your Cave."

"Ah!" said the Cat, listening. "That is a very foolish Dog." And he went back through the Wet Wild Woods waving his wild tail, and walking by his wild lone. But he never told anybody.

When the Man waked up he said, "What is Wild Dog doing here?" And the Woman said, "His name is not Wild

Dog any more, but the First Friend, because he will be our friend for always and always and always. Take him with you when you go hunting."

Next night the Woman cut great green armfuls of fresh grass from the water-meadows, and dried it before the fire, so that it smelt like new-mown hay, and she sat at the mouth of the Cave and plaited a halter out of horse-hide, and she looked at the shoulder of mutton-bone—at the big broad blade-bone—and she made a Magic. She made the Second Singing Magic in the world.

Out in the Wild Woods all the wild animals wondered what had happened to Wild Dog, and at last Wild Horse stamped with his foot and said, "I will go and see and say why Wild Dog has not returned. Cat, come with me."

"Nenni!" said the Cat. "I am the Cat who walks by himself, and all places are alike to me. I will not come." But all the same he followed Wild Horse softly, very softly, and hid himself where he could hear everything.

When the Woman heard Wild Horse tripping and stumbling on his long mane, she laughed and said, "Here comes the second. Wild Thing out of the Wild Woods, what do you want?"

Wild Horse said, "O my Enemy and Wife of my Enemy, where is Wild Dog?"

The Woman laughed, and picked up the blade-bone and looked at it, and said, "Wild Thing out of the Wild Woods, you did not come here for Wild Dog, but for the sake of this good grass."

And Wild Horse, tripping and stumbling on his long mane, said, "That is true; give it me to eat."

The Woman said, "Wild Thing out of the Wild Woods,

bend your wild head and wear what I give you, and you shall eat the wonderful grass three times a day."

"Ah," said the Cat, listening, "this is a clever Woman, but she is not so clever as I am."

Wild Horse bent his wild head, and the Woman slipped the plaited hide halter over it, and Wild Horse breathed on the Woman's feet and said, "Oh my Mistress, and Wife of my Master, I will be your servant for the sake of the wonderful grass."

"Ah," said the Cat, listening, "that is a very foolish Horse." And he went back through the Wet Wild Woods, waving his wild tail and walking by his wild lone. But he never told anybody.

When the Man and the Dog came back from hunting, the Man said, "What is Wild Horse doing here?" And the Woman said, "His name is not Wild Horse any more, but the First Servant, because he will carry us from place to place for always and always and always. Ride on his back when you go hunting."

Next day, holding her wild head high that her wild horns should not catch in the wild trees, Wild Cow came up to the Cave, and the Cat followed, and hid himself just the same as before; and everything happened just the same as before; and the Cat said the same things as before, and when Wild Cow had promised to give her milk to the Woman every day in exchange for the wonderful grass, the Cat went back through the Wet Wild Woods waving his wild tail and walking by his wild lone, just the same as before. But he never told anybody. And when the Man and the Horse and the Dog came home from hunting and asked the same questions as before, the Woman said, "Her name is not Wild Cow any more, but the Giver of Good Food. She will give us the warm white milk for always and always and always, and I will take care of her while you and the First Friend and the First Servant go hunting."

Next day the Cat waited to see if any other Wild thing would go up to the Cave, but no one moved in the Wet Wild Woods, so the Cat walked there by himself; and he saw the Woman milking the Cow, and he saw the light of the fire in the Cave, and he smelt the smell of the warm white milk.

Cat said, "O my Enemy and Wife of my Enemy, where did Wild Cow go?"

The Woman laughed and said, "Wild Thing out of the Wild Woods, go back to the Woods again, for I have braided up my hair, and I have put away the magic blade-bone, and we have no more need of either friends or servants in our Cave."

Cat said, "I am not a friend, and I am not a servant. I am the Cat who walks by himself, and I wish to come into your cave."

Woman said, "Then why did you not come with First Friend on the first night?"

Cat grew very angry and said, "Has Wild Dog told tales of me?"

Then the Woman laughed and said, "You are the Cat who walks by himself, and all places are alike to you. You are neither a friend nor a servant. You have said it yourself. Go away and walk by yourself in all places alike."

Then Cat pretended to be sorry and said, "Must I never come into the Cave? Must I never sit by the warm fire? Must I never drink the warm white milk? You are very wise and very beautiful. You should not be cruel even to a Cat."

Woman said, "I knew I was wise, but I did not know I was beautiful. So I will make a bargain with you. If ever I say one word in your praise you may come into the Cave."

"And if you say two words in my praise?" said the Cat.

"I never shall," said the Woman, "but if I say two words in your praise, you may sit by the fire in the Cave."

"And if you say three words?" said the Cat.

"I never shall," said the Woman, "but if I say three words in your praise, you may drink the warm white milk three times a day for always and always and always."

Then the Cat arched his back and said, "Now let the Curtain at the mouth of the Cave, and the Fire at the back of the Cave, and the Milk-pots that stand beside the Fire, remember what my Enemy and the Wife of my Enemy has said." And he went away through the Wet Wild Woods waving his wild tail and walking by his wild lone.

That night when the Man and the Horse and the Dog came home from hunting, the Woman did not tell them of the bargain that she had made with the Cat, because she was afraid that they might not like it.

Cat went far and far away and hid himself in the Wet Wild Woods by his wild lone for a long time till the Woman forgot all about him. Only the Bat—the little upside-down Bat—that hung inside the Cave, knew where Cat hid; and every evening Bat would fly to Cat with news of what was happening.

One evening Bat said, "There is a Baby in the Cave. He is new and pink and fat and small, and the Woman is very fond of him."

"Ah," said the Cat, listening, "but what is the Baby fond of?"

"He is fond of things that are soft and tickle," said the Bat. "He is fond of warm things to hold in his arms when he goes to sleep. He is fond of being played with. He is fond of all those things."

"Ah," said the Cat, listening, "then my time has come."

Next night Cat walked through the Wet Wild Woods and hid very near the Cave till morning-time, and Man and Dog and Horse went hunting. The Woman was busy cooking that morning, and the Baby cried and interrupted. So she carried him outside the Cave and gave him a handful of pebbles to play with. But still the Baby cried.

Then the Cat put out his paddy paw and patted the Baby on the cheek, and it cooed; and the Cat rubbed against its fat knees and tickled it under its fat chin with his tail. And the Baby laughed; and the Woman heard him and smiled.

Then the Bat—the little upside-down Bat—that hung in the mouth of the Cave said, "O my Hostess and Wife of my Host and Mother of my Host's Son, a Wild Thing from the Wild Woods is most beautifully playing with your Baby."

"A blessing on that Wild Thing whoever he may be," said the Woman, straightening her back, "for I was a busy woman this morning and he has done me a service."

That very minute and second, Best Beloved, the dried horse-skin Curtain that was stretched tail-down at the mouth of the Cave fell down—*whoosh!*—because it remembered the bargain she had made with the Cat, and when the Woman went to pick it up—lo and behold!—the Cat was sitting quite comfy inside the Cave.

"O my Enemy and Wife of my Enemy and Mother of my Enemy," said the Cat, "it is I: for you have spoken a word in my praise, and now I can sit within the Cave for always and always and always. But still I am the Cat who walks by himself, and all places are alike to me."

The Woman was very angry, and shut her lips tight and took up her spinning-wheel and began to spin.

But the Baby cried because the Cat had gone away, and the Woman could not hush it, for it struggled and kicked and grew black in the face.

"O my Enemy and Wife of my Enemy and Mother of my Enemy," said the Cat, "take a strand of the wire that you are spinning and tie it to your spinning-whorl and drag it along the floor, and I will show you a magic that shall make your Baby laugh as loudly as he is now crying."

"I will do so," said the Woman, "because I am at my wits' end; but I will not thank you for it."

She tied the thread to the little clay spindle-whorl and drew it across the floor, and the Cat ran after it and patted it with his paws and rolled head over heels, and tossed it backward over his shoulder and chased it between his hind-legs and pretended to lose it, and pounced down upon it again, till the Baby laughed as loudly as it had been crying, and scrambled after the Cat and frolicked all over the Cave till it grew tired and settled down to sleep with the Cat in its arms.

"Now," said the Cat, "I will sing the Baby a song that shall keep him asleep for an hour." And he began to purr, loud and low, low and loud, till the Baby fell fast asleep. The Woman smiled as she looked down upon the two of them and said, "That was wonderfully done. No question but you are very clever, O Cat."

That very minute and second, Best Beloved, the smoke of the fire at the back of the Cave came down in clouds from the roof—*puff!*—because it remembered the bargain she had made with the Cat, and when it had cleared away—lo and behold!—the Cat was sitting quite comfy close to the fire.

"O my Enemy and Wife of my Enemy and Mother of my Enemy," said the Cat, "it is I, for you have spoken a second word in my praise, and now I can sit by the warm fire at the back of the Cave for always and always and always.

Then the Woman was very very angry, and let down her hair and put more wood on the fire and brought out the broad blade-bone of the shoulder of mutton and began to make a Magic that should prevent her from saying a third word in praise of the Cat. It was not a Singing Magic, Best Beloved, it was a Still Magic; and by and by the Cave grew so still that a little wee-wee mouse crept out of a corner and ran across the floor.

"O my Enemy and Wife of my Enemy and Mother of my Enemy," said the Cat, "is that little mouse part of your magic?"

"Ouh! Chee! No indeed!" said the Woman, and she dropped the blade-bone and jumped upon the footstool in front of the fire and braided up her hair very quick for fear that the mouse should run up it.

"Ah," said the Cat, watching, "then the mouse will do me no harm if I eat it?"

"No," said the Woman, braiding up her hair, "eat it quickly and I will ever be grateful to you."

Cat made one jump and caught the little mouse, and the Woman said, "A hundred thanks. Even the First Friend is not quick enough to catch little mice as you have done. You must be very wise."

That very moment and second, O Best Beloved, the Milk-pot that stood by the fire cracked in two pieces—*ffft*—because it remembered the bargain she had made with the

Cat, and when the Woman jumped down from the footstool —lo and behold!—the Cat was lapping up the warm white milk that lay in one of the broken pieces.

"O my Enemy and Wife of my Enemy and Mother of my Enemy," said the Cat, "it is I; for you have spoken three words in my praise, and now I can drink the warm white milk three times a day for always and always and always. But *still* I am the Cat who walks by himself, and all places are alike to me."

Then the Woman laughed and set the Cat a bowl of the warm white milk and said, "O Cat, you are as clever as a man, but remember that your bargain was not made with the Man or the Dog, and I do not know what they will do when they come home."

"What is that to me?" said the Cat. "If I have my place in the Cave by the fire and my warm white milk three times a day I do not care what the Man or the Dog can do."

That evening when the Man and the Dog came into the Cave, the Woman told them all the story of the bargain while the Cat sat by the fire and smiled. Then the Man said, "Yes, but he has not made a bargain with *me* or with all proper Men after me." Then he took off his two leather boots and he took up his little stone axe (that makes three) and he fetched a piece of wood and a hatchet (that is five altogether), and he set them out in a row and he said, "Now we will make *our* bargain. If you do not catch mice when you are in the Cave for always and always and always, I will throw these five things at you whenever I see you, and so shall all proper Men do after me."

"Ah," said the Woman, listening, "this is a very clever Cat, but he is not so clever as my Man."

The Cat counted the five things (and they looked very

knobby) and he said, "I will catch mice when I am in the Cave for always and always and always; but *still* I am the Cat who walks by himself, and all places are alike to me."

"Not when I am near," said the Man. "If you had not said that last I would have put all these things away for always and always and always; but I am now going to throw my two boots and my little stone axe (that makes three) at you whenever I meet you. And so shall all proper Men after me!"

Then the Dog said, "Wait a minute. He has not made a bargain with *me* or with all proper Dogs after me." And he showed his teeth and said, "If you are not kind to the Baby while I am in the Cave for always and always and always, I will hunt you till I catch you, and when I catch you I will bite you. And so shall all proper Dogs do after me."

"Ah," said the Woman, listening, "this is a very clever Cat, but he is not so clever as the Dog."

Cat counted the Dog's teeth (and they looked very pointed) and he said, "I will be kind to the Baby while I am in the Cave, as long as he does not pull my tail too hard, for always and always and always. But *still* I am the Cat that walks by himself, and all places are alike to me."

"Not when I am near," said the Dog. "If you had not said that last I would have shut my mouth for always and always and always; but *now* I am going to hunt you up a tree whenever I meet you. And so shall all proper Dogs do after me."

Then the Man threw his two boots and his little stone axe (that makes three) at the Cat, and the Cat ran out of the Cave and the Dog chased him up a tree; and from that day to this, Best Beloved, three proper Men out of five will always throw things at a Cat whenever they meet him, and all proper

Dogs will chase him up a tree. But the Cat keeps his side of the bargain too. He will kill mice and he will be kind to Babies when he is in the house, just as long as they do not pull his tail too hard. But when he has done that, and between times, and when the moon gets up and night comes, he is the Cat that walks by himself, and all places are alike to him. Then he goes out to the Wet Wild Woods or up the Wet Wild Trees or on the Wet Wild Roofs, waving his wild tail and walking by his wild lone.

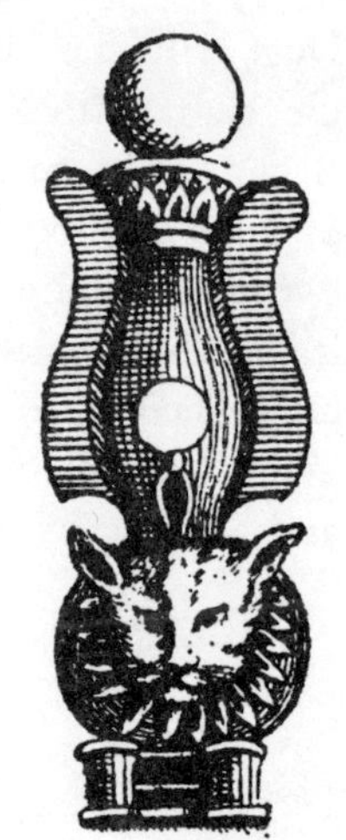

FROM GOD TO DEMON

The cat has played a role in man's religious beliefs as well as in his superstitions for a long time. From ancient Egypt, where the cat was first domesticated and honored for keeping rats from the grain—and then later revered and adored as a god—to twentieth-century Japan, where cats are housed in temples, the animal has had its place in religious rituals. Often that place has been a minor one; for while cats were once considered to be benevolent deities that could confer health, happiness, and wealth upon the faithful, they eventually came to be looked upon as devils capable of perpetrating evil and of inflicting grave harm on unsuspecting humans. Fortunately for the survival of the cat, the cycles of love and hate have generally balanced out—and today the cat maintains its position as a respected, but rarely feared, member of the animal community.

In times past, cats have usually been more prominent in man's superstitions than in his religions. Man has credited the cat with bringing both good luck and bad luck; and the animal has often been thought to be magical itself or, at least, to be responsible for magical or mysterious events. But whether as god or demon, the cat has held an important place in the minds of men of many countries and eras.

The personality traits of the cat are similar to those which human beings in ancient days ascribed to their various gods. The cat is aloof and dignified, at times loving, at times cruel. But most important, the cat has a mysterious air about it, a nature which is not quite understandable. This is very unlike the dog, which is generally a loyal and faithful companion to man unless it has been maltreated.

Ancient peoples held their gods in awe. Because they did not understand science and nature as we do today, they assumed that the "mysteries" of life were known only to the gods. In order to explain the workings of the universe, men invented great myths and legends about powerful deities who controlled human fate and destiny. Parts of these stories incorporated the cat as a god.

RELIGIOUS BELIEFS

One early Greek myth provides a good clue to why the cat was originally worshiped in ancient Egypt. The Greeks told the story of the flight of their gods to Egypt to escape the horrible monster Typhon. Zeus, the chief god, fled disguised as a ram; Apollo the sun god was disguised as a crow; Hermes the messenger as an ibis; Aphrodite the goddess of love as a fish; Ares the god of war as a boar; and Artemis the moon goddess fled to Egypt disguised as a cat. It seems appropriate that the moon goddess took the form of a cat, since the cat's eyes glow in semidarkness and are often thought to resemble the moon. One ancient scholar even stated as a fact that the waxing and waning of the moon were reflected in the widening and closing of a cat's eyes.

While this myth of the Greek religion was popular at a much later time than the cult of the cat in Egypt, it seems logical to assume that since Greek historians recounted it as a very ancient religious legend, the two early cultures had become intertwined and so had the history of their gods. In that case, the gods in their symbolic forms may have originally sprung from primitive cults which first attempted to give meaning to the unexplainable nature of the universe.

The cat was an animal of adoration, worshiped as a god in ancient Egypt. There the cat achieved a status it has never again equaled as the central figure in the cult of Bast (also called Pasht, Bastet, or Basht) at Bubastis, a town which is now a ruin in the lower valley of the Nile River. The earliest pictorial representation of Bast dates from *c.* 3000 B.C. Bast was a cat-headed female goddess. Later associations and superstitions which have linked women with cats probably have their origins in the worship of this goddess, which reached its height in the Twenty-Second Dynasty, around 950 B.C. Originally Bast was a lion-headed goddess, but in her most popular phase she appears with the head of a handsome Egyptian cat. One version of her name, Pasht, may have given rise through the centuries to our familiar "puss."

Bast was the goddess of motherhood, of fertility, of happiness, and of pleasure—all things which can be easily associated with the nature of cats. The animals are usually good mothers; they can have frequent litters of kittens; they are sensitive to luxury and to warmth and to comfortable environments; and furthermore they move with extraordinary grace and beauty, qualities associated with attractive women.

Bast was probably the Egyptian forerunner of the Greek goddess Artemis or the Roman goddess Diana. Both Artemis and Diana were goddesses of the moon. But Bast was also connected with the sun. The cat is an appropriate representation for the Egyptian deity in both her moon and sun guises, since the animal grows more active with the moon and enjoys lying in the sun.

As a god, the cat enjoyed divine protection. Egyptians were forbidden, on pain of death, to harm a cat or to send one out of the country. Cats were extraordinarily well fed; they had the run of Egyptian grain storehouses—obviously because their use as ratters had been appreciated early in their history. Egyptians believed that cats had the power to protect them from evil of all kinds, and craftsmen made bracelets in the form of small cat figures and amulets shaped like kittens and cats to be worn on a chain around the neck. Even young children wore such jewelry to keep "evil spirits" at bay. Sometimes ivory wands or batons surmounted with cats' heads were buried with Egyptian corpses, probably to ensure that on the long, perilous journey to the resting place of the dead the deceased would not be bothered by scorpions, which cats were good at catching.

Egyptians called the cat *mîw,* although some people say that their name was *myeo* or *mau* (the latter means "to see"). Any of the three names are very good representations of the cat's voice.

Statues of mîw show a slim, sleek animal which often had

a scarab carved in its breast and an earring in one ear. One representation shows a cat with a lotus-blossom necklace suspended from a collar; other pictures or statues show cats with necklaces of precious stones. The Egyptian god-cat looked very much like Abyssinian cats of today. In fact, many people think the Abyssinian may be a direct descendant of the cats which lived two or three thousand years before Christ. There are other pictorial versions of Egyptian cats in which the creatures have markings very like our tabby cats—the fur on the forehead is lightly marked with the letter *M*. Perhaps that marking, which is seen on tabbies today, is another reason for the cat's early name of mîw.

Other Egyptian artwork depicts cats as rather wild-looking beasts. In one tomb painting at Deir el Medineh there is a picture of Ra, the Egyptian sun-god, in the form of a cat. The cat-god is holding aloft a knife, ready to cut off the head of an evil serpent which keeps the sun from traveling to the world of the dead. Some frescoes show cats hunting ducks and birds, and two different illustrations on papyrus show a dead woman pouring an offering at an altar on which a dog, a snake, and a cat-god stand, while another papyrus contains a humorous picture of cats and mice in battle—the mice are winning.

Perhaps the earliest picture of a cat is one in the Tomb of Ti which dates from around 2600 B.C. The cat is wearing a collar.

When a cat died in Egypt, the family who owned it often shaved off their eyebrows as a mark of mourning. The family saw to it that their cat was mummified—wrapped in spices and linens—and that a head was carved with eyes and ears which resembled the dead animal's. Then a grand funeral procession, with much loud public weeping and lamenting, carried the mummy to a tomb where it was carefully deposited so that the cat's soul would have a peaceful passage to the world of the dead. Often the mummy was encased in a bronze or gold casket in much the same manner as the ancient Pharoahs were buried. Saucers of food and favorite playthings were left for the cat, and carved effigies of sacred cats were left to guard the mummy. Nothing seems to have been too good for a deceased pet cat.

Public funerals for cats who lived in temples dedicated to Bast must have been wondrous spectacles. The public must have lamented and wept aloud for days and put on a display of adoration and festivity that would make it hard for us to believe that the cause was the death of a cat.

In the late 1800's, 300,000 cat mummies were uncovered at Beni Hassan in Egypt; this was concrete proof of the esteem in which Egyptian cats were held. One of the great tragedies of the science of archaeology is that a merchant in Alexandria, Egypt, shipped most of these mummies to Liverpool, England, in 1890, and the cargo was sold to farmers for fertilizer. Fortunately, a few hundred other cat mummies have been discovered since then, some in Thebes. And from these mummies archaeologists have been able to learn more about the ancient cult of the cat and also about the physical structure of early cats.

The Greeks of antiquity did not worship the cat as the Egyptians did. But some famous Greek writers mentioned the cat, mostly in connection with Egypt. Plutarch, the historian who lived from approximately A.D. 46 to A.D. 120, wrote that Egyptians believed that a male cat represented the sun and a female cat was a symbolic goddess of the moon. Plutarch also commented on the belief, held by Egyptians, Greeks, and many other peoples, that cats are both good and evil.

A Greek orator and writer, Demetrius Phalereus, made the odd statement that a cat's body increased or decreased in size in accordance with the waxing or waning of the moon. It is hard to believe now that people once actually considered such an extraordinary statement to be a "fact" about cats. Even the Egyptians' frenzied adoration seems more logical.

The belief that a cat has nine lives may spring from ancient pagan Greek myths. Cats do have excellent physical coordination and muscular control, which frequently account for their remarkable ability to survive dangerous falls and to survive many near-fatal accidents. To a superstitious people such as the ancient Greeks, this ability of a cat probably seemed to border on magic.

Ancient Greeks also believed that in the beginning of the world the sun and the moon created all the animals. The sun created the lion, and the moon created the cat. Also, in relation to the moon, the Greeks believed that the scuffling gray clouds of early evening were mice which were chased off by the flicking paws of the shining cat of the moon as night progressed.

Greek traders, who were well aware of Egyptian laws against the exporting of cats, made a lucrative business of smuggling the precious beasts into other countries. Together with Phoenician traders and some not-so-religious Egyptians, they established the cat's presence in other Middle Eastern and Asian countries. By the first century of the Christian era, cats were beginning to appear more frequently throughout the known world.

The Etruscans, some of the early civilized peoples in Italy, owned pet cats. But for some unexplained reason, the cat has never in history achieved as revered a status in Western countries as it did in Eastern ones.

Although Julius Caesar was a notorious cat hater, his Roman troops were probably responsible for bringing the domestic cat into Europe and especially into Britain. There might have been some earlier cat arrivals which were transported on Phoenician ships that came to trade in tin with the early residents of Cornwall in England. There is early pictorial evidence of the cat in Roman towns in France, and in Holland there was a Roman town or fort called Cat Vicense, which is known today as cat's town or Kattewyk.

That the Romans did not have the same reverence for cats as the Egyptians is shown by the story of the Roman soldier in Egypt who was accused by a crowd of accidentally murdering a cat. Egyptians, whenever they found a dead cat, would rush away howling mournfully to show that they regretted the loss of the animal and that they had nothing to do with its death. Perhaps the soldier did not understand the custom, but he was savagely attacked and murdered in the streets of Alexandria, and the incident started an Egyptian rebellion against Rome.

Even though the Romans did not worship the cat, it was highly respected as a mouser. At the death of a house cat, some people have said Romans shaved off their eyebrows as a mark of grief, although this may be a confusion with Egyptian customs.

Cats were familiar as designs on Roman flags and banners, and the Roman goddess of liberty was shown with a cat lying comfortably at her feet. The Temple of Liberty put up by the Roman Emperor Tiberius Gracchus was adorned with an image of a cat. The independence of the cat leads to its use as a symbol of liberty. Roman legions which set out to "defend their freedom" had cats blazoned on shields and banners. The cat makes a splendid emblem of freedom because, more than any other animal, it hates to be confined against its will.

Demeter, the Roman goddess of grain and the harvest, occasionally took the form of a cat, perhaps because cats were used to keep grain—a staple of life—free from rats. Diana, the Roman goddess of the moon, had the ability to change herself into a cat in various legends.

Shortly before the birth of Jesus, various Egyptian rites were introduced into pagan Rome, and one of these was the worship of the Egyptian goddess Isis. In a small town near Vesuvius, Italy, paintings were found of the Roman rites of Isis, which included a sistrum, a musical instrument that was shaken like a rattle to frighten away evil spirits, on the top of which is a carved cat's head.

Later Italian Christian legends concern the child Jesus and a kitten. It is said that at the moment Jesus was born in the stable of Bethlehem, a mother cat lying below the manger gave birth to a kitten.

One of the ancient beliefs held both in Burma and in Siam was that the soul of a person who had attained a high degree of spirituality entered the body of a cat when the person died. The soul stayed within the cat's body until the animal died. This was, more or less, a temporary purgatory, for the soul could only pass into paradise by this means.

In Burma in the 1700's, an order of monks living in an underground cave called The Abode of the Gods (*Lao-*

Tsun) had sacred cats which played a prominent part in ceremonies. A hundred Burmese cats lived in the temple and were considered holy. One special cat with large golden eyes sat at the foot of a statue of the order's goddess with his master, an elderly high priest. The cat and man seem to have spent their days in contemplation of the statue. This cat was also supposed to be an oracle which could impart wisdom, and the priest consulted the cat-oracle on decisions of any importance.

Cats in Siam have also taken part in religious rituals. In various temples, silken black-coated animals with huge golden eyes were and still are often kept in cages adorned with gold leaf, where they lie on cushions with offerings of incense and food from the priests and the faithful before them.

The Siamese cat, a breed that is very popular today, has a shadowy patch on the back of its neck. A Siamese legend says that a god once picked up such a cat by the scruff of its neck, and forever after the shadow of the god's hand appeared on descendants of that Siamese cat.

Another interesting Siamese belief was that a live cat should be buried with the body of any deceased member of royalty. The tomb was pierced with small holes so that the cat could eventually worm its way free. When it did so, the temple priests acknowledged that the soul of the dead member of royalty had passed into the cat's body, and the cat was led to the temple with great ceremony.

When the heir to the Siamese throne was crowned in 1926, a cat was carried ceremoniously by members of the court into the throne room for the coronation. The cat was supposedly carrying the soul of the king who had just died.

The cat stands as a symbol of self-possession, a much-desired character trait in Chinese Buddhism. Buddhists also have believed that a cat whose coat was light-colored would bring silver to his owners, whereas a cat with a dark-colored coat would bring gold.

According to an ancient story, when the Buddha died, the cat was the only animal barred from attending the funeral, for the cat was said to have caught and eaten the rat which had gone to get medicine to help cure the Buddha.

In the *Li-Ki,* or Chinese *Book of Rites,* there is a passage which tells of Chinese farmers worshiping a cat called Li Shou. When the crops were safely harvested, the farmers and their families held festivals and made sacrifices to the cat-god for killing and eating mice which could have destroyed the crops.

In some regions of China in very ancient times a spirit in the form of a cat was worshiped because of its much-desired ability to see in the dark. Evil spirits were more prevalent at night, and because of cats' excellent eyesight, the animals were thought to be able to detect the unwanted and fearsome demons. Pictures of cats were pasted on Chinese houses to ward off evil spirits. Cat pictures were also used to scare off rats from silk-worm colonies, if live cats couldn't be procured as guards.

The ancient Chinese dreaded and feared a beast which was a "cat-specter." The people believed that women often served these demons, and this belief may partially account for later beliefs that old women served the devil disguised as cats. Cats in the form of specters were supposed to kill humans, and then things of value which had belonged to the deceased were magically drawn to the dwelling place of the demon cat.

About the same time in history, the Chinese also believed that after death some people turned into cat-specters in order to revenge themselves on their enemies.

In Japan, the cat was often believed to have the power to bewitch men and women, and people were terrified of magical cats with forked tails and vampire cats who drained the blood of living people.

Some Japanese religious groups believed that a cat with a black mark on its back contained the soul of someone's deceased ancestor, and such a cat would be taken to a temple to live out its days in comfort and adoration. Japanese fishermen often take a tortoise-shell cat in their boats, for they believe such a cat will protect them from the ghosts of their ancestors.

There is an old legend which explains the fondness of the Japanese for a good-luck charm in the form of a sitting cat with a paw raised to ear level—the "beckoning cat" charm. Once the temple of Gotoku-ji was very poor and attended only by poor monks, their chief priest, and a faithful cat. One day, as the cat was sitting in the yard, some noble Samurai warriors rode by on horseback. The cat looked at the horsemen and raised its paw to its ear, appearing to be beckoning them. The warriors stopped and followed the cat to the poor temple. A heavy rain fell, and they stayed in the shelter of the temple, where the chief priest gave them tea and talked about the way of Buddhism. After that incident, one of the Samurai named Li returned to the temple for instruction in the faith, and eventually he endowed and rebuilt the poor temple magnificently. There is still a small shrine to the "beckoning cat" in the grounds of the temple outside Tokyo today. Visitors go there to pray for good luck and prosperity, assured that the little cat will be able to summon good fortune.

The Crusaders brought many more cats back to Europe after their travels to the east to wrest the holy places from the "nonbelievers." And so the domestic cat population spread widely into the European countries. The Middle Ages, stretching from approximately the fifth century A.D. to the sixteenth century, saw the adoration of cats decline quickly with the spread of Christianity. The cat became a creature to be feared and tormented because of its supposed connection with Satan and witches—enemies of God and the Christian religion as well as servants of the Devil.

In the fifteenth century, the cat came as close to extinction as it ever has in its long history. A Teutonic cult grew up in the Rhineland which centered around the Norse Goddess Freya, whose chariot was drawn by two black cats. As this cult flourished so did the popularity of black cats. But critics felt that Christianity was being undermined by the popularity of the wild pagan rites associated with Freya, and the persecution was on. Two popes of the century, Sixtus IV and Innocent VIII, instituted laws which allowed the torture of suspected cult members and suspected witches—this of course included black cats by association as animal "familiars."

Witch hunts abounded. For hundreds of years, humans and their animals were senselessly tortured and killed when mass hysteria reigned. Often a person was considered a witch merely because of possession of a cat. A poem written by John Gay (1685–1732), the English author of *The Beggar's Opera,* illustrates this "guilt by association."

The Old Woman and Her Cats

by John Gay, from *Fables*

A wrinkled hag, of wicked fame
Beside a little smoky flame
Sat Hov'ring, pinched with age and frost;
Her shrivell'd hands, with veins embossed, . . .

About her swarm'd a num'rous brood
Of Cats, who lank with hunger mew'd.
Teaz'd with their cries her choler grew,
And thus she sputter'd. Hence, ye crew.
Fool that I was to entertain
Such imps, such fiends, a hellish train!
Had ye been never hous'd and nurs'd
I, for a witch, had ne'er been curs'd.
To you I owe, that crowds of boys
Worry me with eternal noise;
Straws laid across my pace retard,
The horse-shoe's nail'd (each threshold's guard).
The stunted broom the wenches hide,
For fear that I should up and ride. . . .

Replies a Cat. Let's come to proof.
Had we ne'er starved beneath your roof
We had, like others of our race,
In credit liv'd, as beasts of chase.
'Tis infamy to serve a hag;
And boys against our lives combine,
Because, 'tis said, your cats have nine.

The superstitious belief that a cat had nine lives was referred to in connection with witches in a book of 1584 called *Beware of the Cat*. The author stated that "it was permitted to a witch to take on her catte's body nine times." One of the most persistent beliefs in the Middle Ages was that if the Devil heard Jesus' name spoken aloud, he would run off in the form of a black cat.

The famous Scottish witch, Isobel Gowdrie, was put on trial in 1662 and under examination told her accusers the spell which she and her followers used to change themselves into cats:

> I shall goe intill ane catt,
> With sorrow, and sych, and a blak shott;
> And I sall goe in the Devillis nam,
> Ay guhill I com home again.

The last two lines of the spell must have struck a chill in the hearts of her judges, for that was "concrete" proof that she did the Devil's, not God's, work in the form of a cat. Other witches and warlocks in her coven, or group, which had agreed to serve the Devil, could change each other into cats at will, they claimed.

The fear of witches' cats obviously arose from the animals' ancient association with Artemis the moon goddess. In Patricia Dale-Green's book, *Cult of the Cat,* she writes: "Gods of an earlier religion become demons in the cult that supersedes it." Artemis, the moon goddess, in Roman times was called Diana; Diana was also goddess of the dark. It was Diana who, according to an ancient myth, sent Aradia (first of all the witches) to earth to teach human beings magic and witchcraft.

Eventually the Christian witch hysteria crossed the Atlantic. In Salem Village, Massachusetts, scene of the infamous Salem witchcraft trials, cats were thought to be agents of the devil. Cats are mentioned in the official documents of the trials which are on record in Essex County, Massachusetts.

In the March 1, 1691–92 evidence against Tituba Indian and Sarah Good, two women accused of witchcraft, there appears a summary of Tituba's testimony:

> ". . . she further saith that she saw a cat with good [Sarah Good] at another time."

and again:

> "Saw Good have a Cat besides the bird . . ."

and in later testimony on March 7, 1691–92:

> . . . the said John Hughes being in Bed in a closed Room and the door being fast so that no cat nor dog could come in the said John Saw a Great light appear in the said Chamber and Rising up in his bed he saw a large Gray Cat at his bed's foot.

Robert Downer's testimony of June 30, 1692, against the accused witch Susanna Martin must have struck terror in the hearts of the Puritans who sat listening:

> she . . . said that a she devil would fetch him away shortly at which this deponent was not much moved but at night as he lay in his bed in his own house alone there came at his window the likeness of a cat and by and by come up to

> his bed took fast hold of his throat and Lay hard upon him a Considerable while and was like to throttle him at Length he minded what Susanna Martin had threatened him with the Day before he strove what he could and said avoid thou she devil in the name of the father and the son and the holy Ghost and then it Let him go and slumped down upon the floor and went out at window again.

In the 1700's the persecution for witchcraft declined and, as a result, the cat again rose in favor as a domestic animal. Since the eighteenth century, the animal has gained steadily in popularity and affection, but it has never since really been thought to be either God or Demon.

SUPERSTITIOUS BELIEFS

Ever since ancient Egyptians worshiped the cat, people have believed many exaggerated things about the animal. Many of the cat superstitions arose from early connections with religious practices, and many others arose from physical observations of the way a cat moves and behaves.

A superstition is an irrational fear or irrational reverence for a mysterious or supernatural or unknown thing. For thousands of years men knew very little about the events or actions they witnessed either in the skies or on earth, and so they naturally tended to invent explanations which now seem preposterous. The cat was, and is, an unusual and perplexing animal. The superstitions about cats are so numerous that an entire book could be written about them.

Everyone "knows" that if a black cat crosses your path it

means bad luck, or if a white cat follows you home good luck will follow, too. Some people believe that all cats are bad in May or that May kittens are always troublesome. Certainly most young women would like to believe that whoever cares well for a cat will marry as happily as she could wish.

No one knows for sure just where and when all these superstitions arose or how widespread the belief in them was, or is. But the superstitious beliefs are one of the most interesting facets of the history of the cat.

The eyes of the cat, in particular, have always fascinated people. The ancient Chinese believed that you could tell the time of day by carefully watching a cat's eyes. In the morning, its eyes would be wide open with the pupils dilated; toward night, its eyes supposedly would grow smaller and the pupils would appear slitted. Telling time by the appearance of a cat's eyes is not as silly as it sounds. A cat's eyes do enlarge or grow smaller depending upon how much light is present. Cats cannot see in total darkness, although many people still believe that they can.

As late as the seventeenth century, a book called the *Historie of Foure-Footed Beasts,* written by an Englishman, Edmund Topsell, in 1607, recorded:

> The Egyptians have observed in the eyes of the Cat, the encrease of the moonlight for with the Moone, they shine more fully at the ful, and more dimly in the change and wain [the waning of the moon], and the male cat doth vary his eyes with the sunne; for when the sun ariseth, the apple of his eye is long; towards noon it is round, and at the evening it cannot be seene at all, but the whole eye showeth alike.

Edmund Topsell also explained the effect on men of seeing a cat's glowing eyes:

> Here eies [eyes] glister above measure, especially when a man cometh to see a cat on the sudden, and in the night they can hardly be endured for their flaming aspect.

Ancient Britons even believed that if you gazed deeply into a cat's eyes, you would be able to see exactly what was happening in the spirit world.

Superstitions about cats and the weather go far back in history. Cats are notoriously sensitive to changes in weather. Their hair often stands up on end if a lightning storm is approaching. They are very frisky before the first snow fall. They grow restless in early spring, and they are usually languid and lazy in midsummer. Sailors believed that cats could tell if changes in the weather were coming, particularly in bad weather. In Ireland cats were once caught and confined under a big cooking pot if a storm blew up, in the hope that the cat, by being kept prisoner in a small space, would grow calm and thus calm the weather. People have also thought that if a cat winked, rain would fall. Cats have a long history as "rainmakers" and have been used in primitive rituals to bring rain in South America and various Pacific islands.

Because witches were thought to be able to raise terrible storms, cats by association with them were also supposed to be able to create tempests. One of Scotland's most famous witches, Agnes Sampson, actually confessed at her second trial that she had used a cat to bring about a storm in order to shipwreck Queen Anne and King James on their voyage home from Denmark. With evidence like that, it is no wonder that people of the time believed the superstitions about cats and weather.

That cats can bring either good or bad health to people is an old superstition. These beliefs most likely originated from the fact that Bast, the Egyptian cat-goddess, was also a goddess possessing great healing powers. The beliefs may also have been reinforced because of cats being companions of witches. The old women who were accused of witchcraft were often adept at healing human ailments with a variety of herbs and odd potions.

Since ancient Egyptian times people have believed that a white cat can destroy the effects of poison. This belief may have arisen from the fact that cats are fascinated by bugs and probably killed many a deadly Egyptian scorpion before it had a chance to sting either an animal or a human being.

People from many countries have thought that if the tail of a cat were laid against a blind man's eyes, sight would be restored. There is a cure for blindness given in the *Historie of Foure-Footed Beasts:*

> Take the head of a black cat, which hath not a spot of colour in it, and burn it to powder in an earthen pot, leaded or glazed within; then take this powder, and, through a quill, blow it thrice a day into thy eye; and if in the night any heat do thereby annoy thee, take two leaves of an oke, wet in cold water, and bind them to the eye, and so shall all pain flie away, and blindness depart, although it hath oppressed thee a whole year; and this medecine is approved by many physicians both elder and later.

Unfortunately, there is no factual record which proves the last statement in this prescription, so it must be accorded the status of a superstition.

Rubbing a cat's tail across the eyes, some people think, will cure a sty, and an itch will go away if you can rub it with the tail. You can also get rid of warts by rubbing them with a tomcat's tail. Not any cat will do, though; you must use the tail of a tortoiseshell tom.

The cat has often been thought to bring good luck. In fact, the lucky cat is very popular in fairy tales and in legends. One of the most famous is Puss in Boots, who brings his young master good fortune and a pretty bride; and then there is Dick Whittington's cat. He brought wealth and good fortune to the future Lord Mayor of London. Dick Whittington was a real character in history, but whether his lucky cat was real, too, we do not know.

In ancient China, old, ugly cats were kept chained to shops because the merchants were convinced the animals would bring good luck. If the cat escaped, it was believed that business would suffer, for good fortune disappeared with the animal. This Chinese belief is very similar to that of the Japanese who, even today, keep little statues of cats before their shops to bring good fortune.

In Scotland, a cat with a double set of claws was supposed to be the bearer of luck. Maybe people believed this because it seemed that two sets of claws would help a cat catch more rats. Scotsmen also believed that a stray tortoiseshell cat who settled down in a home brought good luck. Many other people besides the Scots believed this, too.

Arabs have believed, since the days before the Islamic religion was established, that a golden cat brought good luck.

Even now, they believe that a cat in either a mosque or a tent signifies the presence of good fortune.

Cats have been thought to bring bad luck, too. A black cat crossing your path meant someone you knew was going to die. The old folklore of Finland tells that black cats were messengers of death and that they also carried the souls of dead people to the other world. People have also believed that if a strange black cat visits a house good luck is coming; but if it wants to stay, then bad luck will come. Perhaps this superstition has some connection with the ancient Finnish belief, for if black cats are death messengers and if they do not stay in a house, then no one is carried away to the resting place of the dead.

There is an old French superstition that it is bad luck to carry a cat across water in your arms. The Devil might get you or you might die. And people in several different countries have believed that it is bad luck for a cat to come into the presence of a person recently deceased—if the cat happened to be a witch in disguise, she might be after your soul. The Germans believed that it was exceptionally bad luck for a sick person to see two cats fighting. The onlooker was almost certain to die as a result.

Southern mountain people in America sometimes believe that if black cats are kept in a house where there are unmarried daughters, all the girls will remain old maids. Southern Frenchmen believe that if an unmarried girl accidentally steps on the tail of a cat, she'll go another year without finding a husband. Many people have also believed that cats can foretell whether or not a wedding will take place. If a cat of any description shows up on the day of your wedding, everything will turn out for the best. This belief has been widely held throughout Europe for hundreds of years.

Undoubtedly most of the superstitions and warnings against cats can be traced to their role as witches' familiars, or companions. In days when people believed firmly in witches and their ability to perform horrible magic, it was only natural that cats who lived with witches should be feared; they might have some of the evil power of their mistresses.

Today, the warning "Beware of the Cat" has faded into insignificance because of the scientific facts. Cats do not possess the ability to perform magic, either good or bad; they do not bewitch human beings or carry their souls after death; and they probably do not bring bad luck. Unfortunately, they probably don't bring good luck either, but it would be pleasant to believe that such a fascinating creature as the cat could be the bearer of fame, fortune, and good health.

FELIS CATUS DOMESTICUS

The domestic cat, whose scientific name is *Felis catus,* has a history which can be traced back in time for nearly 3,500 years. The Egyptians were probably the first people to domesticate the cat, and their early affection and respect for the animal led to the rise of a religious cat cult. There are a few people who think that the cat first might have been tamed in China or in India, but most prefer the theory of Egyptian pet cats.

When did the cat first appear on earth? Scientists are fairly certain that the cat developed from the family Miacidae, one of the first carnivores, which lived approximately fifty million years ago during the Eocene Epoch. The Miacidae were the ancestors of several familiar families of animals: the dog, primarily, but also the hyena, the civet, and the weasel. The

Miacidae, in fact, looked very much like long, ugly weasels. Our domestic cat developed from the civet branch of the Miacidae's descendants, as did other types of feline animals such as the lion, the tiger, and the wildcat. The Miacidae developed into a civet in about ten million years' time.

It took another four million years for the civet to produce another family of felines—the *Dinictis,* an animal which was getting very close to today's cat. The *Dinictis* had some familiar cat characteristics: Its teeth were very catlike, and it had retractable claws. Its body was the size of a lynx, which is bigger than a domestic cat, but the brain was very small. During the Oligocene Epoch, thirty-six million years ago, *Dinictis* was beginning to look very much like a modern cat. Finally, in the Pleistocene Epoch, during the last million years of the Stone Age, man appeared on the earth, and so did around forty species of feline animals, including *Felis catus.*

Throughout the thousands of years since the cat first appeared in its present form, it has managed to remain the same in form and shape—except for one exceedingly rare hairless mutant which is an offspring of the curly coated Rex breed of cats. If an inhabitant of the earth were to point out a cat to a visitor from another planet, the visitor would certainly be able to recognize all other pet cats on sight whether they were highly bred Persians, delicate Siamese, alley cats, or even the tailless Manx cats. The same would not be true of dogs. Space visitors would have a difficult time recognizing a St. Bernard and a dachshund as members of the same family.

Even though cats of different breeds look more or less alike, it is very difficult to trace their genealogy directly. Domestic cats in Europe and America are certainly part wildcat, and, although it is not frequent any more, in years past when wildcats were not rare, domestic cats often "reverted" or went back to the wild state and mated with wildcats.

One type of cat, the *Persian,* is fairly easy to trace, although part of its history may be legend. King Cambyses of Persia conquered Egypt in 525 B.C. When the Persian army went home they took with them some of the sacred Egyptian cats. The climate in Persia was considerably colder than the mild weather in Egypt, and so through the generations Persian or Angora cats began developing longer and thicker fur to protect them from the cold. The Persians themselves were conquered in 331 B.C. by Alexander the Great, and the Persian court fled, with their prized cats, to the Chorassan plateau in the eastern part of their country. Great strongholds were built on the mountainsides there, and for two centuries Persian cats had to adapt to even more extreme weather conditions. This adaptation of the cat was exactly mirrored in the Angora goat and in the rabbits which lived in high mountainous regions. By the year A.D. 247, when the Parthian empire was at its height, the Persian cat had evolved in looks as we know it today, and the animal became a valuable export to foreign countries.

The Persian, or Angora cat as it was first called, was finally imported into Europe in the late sixteenth century. The French scholar and naturalist Nicholas de Peiresc introduced the cat into France, where it was immediately popular, although rare. Long-haired cats have continued in popularity until the present day. In fact, Persians are one of the most popular of all domestic cats.

Tabby cats are probably direct descendants of sacred

Egyptian cats. Their distinctive striped or spotted markings, very like pictures of ancient cats which lived in the Nile River valley. The name tabby is supposed to have come from a bazaar district of Baghdad, called Attābi. In the bazaar, watered silk was sold, which was considered a luxury by ladies of fashion in Europe; the silk had markings that were much like our tabby cats' markings. The silk was called "tabbi," and the similarity to the cat's markings led to the animal's name—"tabby."

Birman cats used to be sacred in ancient Burma. These seal or blue cats with darker-brown masks, much like the Siamese, and bushy tails, were kept in temples by the priests of Burma. The first pair of Burmese cats arrived in Europe in 1919. They were sent as a present of thanks to British Major Gordon Russell who had helped to put down a local uprising and enabled a few priests to escape from Burma into Tibet in 1916.

The *Abyssinian* cat was first introduced into Europe more than a hundred years ago from its native Abyssinia. It is a regal-looking cat, slim in body with a long face, and its coat is fawn-colored with black and dark-brown tick markings. Although it has been considerably changed by breeding, the cat bears a resemblance to pictures and statues of ancient Egyptian cats, as does the tabby cat.

The *Siamese* cat was an ancient sacred cat of Siam. It has, perhaps, the most distinctive of all appearances: a fawn-colored body with contrasting points (mask, ears, paws and tail); china-blue eyes; and exceptionally long claws. The points are usually in one of four colors: seal (black-brown), blue, chocolate, and lilac. The Siamese also has a fierce, raucous voice, although it does meow and purr like ordinary cats. The Siamese is as popular as the Persian cat, and it needs human companionship and affection more than other felines—a trait that is, of course, endearing to humans.

The *Manx* cat, known as a "rumpy," is tailless or has a very short tail. Show animals must have no tail whatever. Its origin is unknown, although it is thought that the first two landed on the Isle of Man when a ship of the Spanish Armada was wrecked off the coast near Port Erin. One well-traveled explorer named Auguste Pavie believed that Manx cats might have some connection with Annamite cats, which were imported to the East Indies by trading ships from Britain in the eighteenth century. Annamite cats were small and had only very short tails. Whether the Manx cat's lack of a tail is the result of generations of breeding with short-tailed cats, or whether the Manx originally had no tail, no one knows for sure.

There are numerous other special breeds of cats; everyone has his or her favorite. But whether the cat you favor is a highly prized show winner or an alley cat, it is probably descended in one way or another from the sacred cats of the Orient or Africa or from Asian or European wildcats.

The first relative that one thinks of in connection with the domestic cat, *Felis catus,* is the wildcat, *Felis silvestris,* which inhabits a few parts of southern and central Europe and a few areas of northern and central Asia. Occasionally wildcats are discovered in northern Scotland and in France today, but the event is always rare.

The wildcat resembles the pet tabby cat except that its body is a bit heavier. Wildcats have a grayish-yellow fur with black stripes on the flanks, at the sides of the face, and down the middle of the back. Their tails are fluffy and longer than that of domestic cats. Normally, their ears do not stand up as do those of domestic cats, but this may seem true only because whenever the cat has been photographed it is exceptionally afraid and angry.

Wildcats are fierce and violently resist any attempts at domestication. Very few attempts have been successful. They do occasionally mate with pet cats, and the offspring generally revert to the wild.

Although there is a great deal of resemblance between wildcats and domestic cats, biologically they are two quite distinct species, although they belong to the same family, Felidae.

The other relatives which immediately spring to mind are the big members of the family Felidae: the cheetah, the leopard, the lion, the jaguar, the puma, and the tiger. Some less-well-known members of the cat family are the serval and the African Kaffir, or fettered, cat. And even the civet and the hyena are distant relatives of Felidae. The domestic cat has many things in common with its large relatives. First of all, puss looks quite like his other family members, and secondly, the domestic cat moves and behaves in a similar manner, although with less ferocity and on a smaller scale. When one watches a tiger or a lioness playing with her cubs in a zoo, the actions can be seen to be almost a replica of any kindly domesticated mother cat playing with her kittens. A cat lying in wait for a mouse is a smaller version of a tiger crouched ready to spring on its prey.

Cats, big and small, are flesh eaters. All sizes of cats are physically similar. They are lean and agile and have powerful muscles. They all have retractable claws which are strong and needle-sharp, except for the cheetah. All cats see most effectively in semilight, and their hunting is dependent primarily on their keen sight, for their sense of smell is not nearly so well developed as that of the dog. Cats' whiskers are a sensory organ and enable the animals to judge distance and space.

The family relations of the domestic cat are wide-ranging. But so are the relationships of the cat to other animals. Cat and rat, cat and dog, and cat and man are all familiar and old relationships.

The history of cat and rat goes as far back as the cat's own history. Cats were probably first domesticated as a result of their fondness for eating mice and rats. Old legends and proverbs deal with cats and rats; one of the first cat proverbs a child hears is "When the cat's away, the mice will play."

In John Gay's *Fables* there is a wonderful story about a battle between a cat and an employed rat catcher:

The rats by night such mischief did,
Betty was ev'ry morning chid:
They undermin'd whole sides of bacon,
Her cheese was sapp'd, her tarts were taken,
Her pasties, fenc'd with thickest paste,
Were all demolish'd and laid waste.
She curst the cat for want of duty,
Who left her foes a constant booty.
An Engineer, of noted skill,
Engag'd to stop the growing ill.
From room to room he now surveys
Their haunts, their works, their secret ways,
Finds where they 'scape an ambuscade,

And whence the nightly sally's made.
  An envious Cat, from place to place,
Unseen, attends his silent pace,
She saw that if his trade went on,
The purring race must be undone,
So, secretly removes his baits,
And ev'ry stratagem defeats.
  Again he sets the poison'd toils,
And puss again the labour foils.
  What foe (to frustrate my designs)
My schemes thus nightly undermines?
Incens'd, he cries: this very hour
The wretch shall bleed beneath my power.
  So said. A Pond'rous trap he brought,
And in the fact poor puss was caught.
  Smuggler, says he, thou shalt be made
A victim to our loss of trade.
  The captive Cat with piteous mews
For pardon, life and freedom sues.
A sister of the science spare,
One int'rest is our common care.
  What insolence! the man reply'd,
Shall cats with us the game divide?
Were all your interloping band
Extinguish'd, or expell'd the land,
We Rat-catchers might raise our fees,
Sole guardians of a nation's cheese!
  A Cat, who saw the lifted knife,
Thus spoke, and sav'd her sister's life.
  In ev'ry age and clime we see,
Two of a trade can ne'er agree,

Each hates his neighbour for encroaching;
Squire stigmatizes squire for poaching;
Beauties with beauties are in arms,
And scandal pelts each other's charms;
Kings too their neighbour kings dethrone,
In hope to make the world their own.
But let us limit our desires,
Not war like beauties, kings and squires,
For though we both one prey pursue,
There's game enough for us and you.

Much fun has been made of the cat's appetite for the rat. There have been carvings and pictures throughout history of rats getting the better of cats; fairy tales have been written showing humorously how the rat often gets the better of the cat; and in modern times there has been the famous "Tom and Jerry" cartoons in which Tom, the big, fat, evil black-and-white cat is always getting hit over the head or defurred or put outdoors because of the cleverness of the sly little mouse, Jerry.

One poet, George Turberville, who lived from 1540 to 1610, even wrote a poem to a young lady he loved telling how he would protect her from a rat if he were to become a cat:

I would be present, aye,
  And at my Ladie's call;
To gard her from the fearfull Mouse,
  In Parlour and in Hall;
In Kitchen, for his Lyfe,
  He should not shew his head;

The Peare in Poke should lie untoucht
When shee were gone to Bed.
The Mouse should stand in Feare,
So should the squeaking Rat;
And this would I do if I were
Converted to a Cat.

The cat is one of the oldest of our domestic pets—although not so old as the dog. Distressing as the fact may be to cat lovers, the dog has been man's faithful companion for much longer than the cat. The cat has shared the tents and houses of man for only several thousand years, but that is long enough for the creature to implant itself in the mind and imagination of humans.

The enmity between cat and dog has a long, long history too. But if brought up together and well trained, cats and dogs often grow very fond of one another. Strange dogs and cats, it is true, usually despise each other on sight—the dog barks, the cat howls and runs up the nearest tree, with yapping canine in hot pursuit.

Almost all cat people enjoy comparing the qualities of dog and cat—it seems to be a comparison they cannot resist, although the dog's well-known affection for man often puts the cat in a bad light. Alfred Brehm, a German naturalist, made one comparison which seems to judge both the cat and the dog fairly:

> Our domestic cat is an extraordinarily elegant, clean, graceful and lovely creature. Each of her movements is fine and pleasant, and her agility is truly admirable. As a rule people compare her with the dog, with whom she

> should not be compared at all. The dog is not remotely so expressive as the cat.

Brehm's phrase "with whom she should not be compared at all" shows what both cat and dog people know—the dog has its own specially appealing qualities, and so does the cat; it is unfair to both of our favorite domestic pets to say one is more amenable than the other, because it is simply a matter of preference.

Michael Joseph, a publisher and author who was inordinately fond of cats, wrote a very condescending comparison in which the poor dog suffers:

> The dog is, for some, a completely satisfying companion. He is a good, faithful servant, certainly. But in truth he is noisy, clumsy and dirty. He has all the qualities of the peasant. The cat, by contrast, is an aristocrat; reserved, immaculate, graceful, acknowledging no human master. His friendship is not easily won but it is something worth having.

No cat could possibly write a more favorable opinion of its own qualities; it would be an easy thing to imagine that one of Mr. Joseph's cats actually dictated the comparison to him.

In recent years the mind and nature of *Felis catus* have been the subject of scientific study. The I.Q.'s of some cats have been studied—a particularly intelligent Siamese is thought to have an intelligent quotient of perhaps 65 to 75—and so have their physical reactions and their psychological actions. As man progresses in an understanding of man, it helps him to study intelligent domestic pets such as dogs and cats to see if their actions in various situations can be compared to the reactions of men and women in similar situations.

One of the most fascinating areas of cat study is in the field of extrasensory perception. Although cats are primarily home-loving creatures, and once established in a house they usually prefer not to change, there have been many accounts of cats that traveled long distances to find their owners or to find their homes. The fact that cats have often displayed an unerring homing instinct has recently interested scientists and researchers as well as the general public—not just as interesting anecdotes but as an area of scientific inquiry. Of course, other animals besides cats have this so-called "built-in" radar which enables them to return to their homes, and not very much is actually known about the phenomenon. Susy Smith, the author of a book called *ESP,* thinks that the ability of a cat to find his way home may be, in some way, connected with an extrasensory-perception ability—the ability to foresee, in some as yet unexplained way, the route home. Miss Smith tells the following true story of a cat:

> More convincing to many students of extrasensory perception is the ability of domestic animals to find their way back over long distances, sometimes after having been removed from the original location in closed vehicles and by an indirect route. Even more baffling are those human interest accounts of pet cats and dogs left behind or lost when the owners move to a new home. Weeks, months, even a year later these pets, battered and footsore but grimly determined, arrive at the new home—a place they

have never seen before, sometimes hundreds of miles from their former environment.

Such an animal was Old Tom, a member of the Coleman Feldman family which moved seventy-five miles from a Yucalpa, California, ranch to Hollywood on April 14, 1961, leaving him behind. One year later the black cat appeared at the Feldman's Hollywood address. The new owners of the ranch said Old Tom vanished during the summer of 1961. The Feldmans identified him by the scars of his previous battles, and the family dog Candy, who has no use for strange cats, greeted his former pal with great affection.

Whether or not ESP was the factor responsible for Old Tom's remarkable year-long journey, no one can say, but some people feel that there is a good possibility that animals, and especially cats, do possess extrasensory perception. A recent article in the American *Journal of Parapsychology* reported on the results of a scientific experimental project, supported in part by a Rockefeller Foundation grant, to test whether cats had ESP. The researchers attempted to test ESP in cats by putting the animals, one at a time, in an enclosed runway with two cups of food at one end. The experiment was carefully conducted so that the cats could not smell the food and could not see what was in the cups. After laborious testing with numerous cats, the researchers concluded that the incidence of cats choosing the cup with the food in it was high enough to suppose that some factor beyond the ordinary senses of sight, hearing, touch, taste, and smell was operating which permitted cats to make the right choice. The researchers who performed this experiment in the Parapsychology Laboratory of Duke University in Durham, North Carolina, stated as a conclusion to their article: "The present experiment yielded significant results under conditions that make clairvoyance in cats seem the most likely explanation."

Scientific research on cats and other animals to determine whether ESP does exist is going on continually, and there is a chance that in the future a scientist will be able to state definitely that he has proved that cats do possess extrasensory perception. If so, that will be a great scientific advance and will have far-reaching consequences for the human race.

The domestic cat, with a history which is inextricably intertwined with man's, may yet prove to be the most valuable of domestic animals, for through the intelligent cat, man may learn more about himself.

THE CAT FANCY

What is the "cat fancy"? Strictly speaking, the cat fancy is made up of members of those affiliated Cat Clubs and Societies in the U.K. which elect delegates each year to the Governing Council of the Cat Fancy. The G.C.C.F.'s prime objectives are the provision for the registration of cats and of cat pedigrees, the classification of breeds, the approval of dates of cat shows, the improvement of cat breeding and the welfare of cats. The Council also grants Challenge Certificates to winning cats at the Championship Shows held under its auspices and rules, and agree the standards and points scale for breeds.

There are official Cat Clubs and Societies in the Commonwealth countries, there is the Canadian Cat Association, and seven major cat organisations in the U.S. But, the cat fancy is really made up of all people who like, love, adore, admire, or simply fancy cats. And they number hundreds of thousands.

Some Cat Clubs in the U.K. are specialised like the Abyssinian Cat Club or the Chocolate Pointed Siamese Cat Club, while others are general like the Cheshire Area Cat Club or the Kensington Kitten and Neuter Cat Club. In America, the cat fancy has become slightly fanciful which is shown in the naming of the Glitter Gulch Cat Club of Las Vegas or the surprising Crown Jewels Cat Club of Atlanta. That the cat fancy often stretches credulity is evident even in England: of an estimated cat population of 6 million, 100,000 cats are supposed to be "employed" by the Civil Service (journalists often comment on the number of rats which require this work force . . .).

On a more serious note, any cat fancier will enjoy *Cats* magazine, and *Fur and Feather* announces cat show schedules and prints other articles and advertising of interest to those who show, breed or simply fancy felines.

All in all, the cat holds a very important place in society today. Some companies' entire business is given over to manufacturing and selling cat foods and cat toys and jeweled cat collars and harnesses. There are special cat veterinarians and even cat psychiatrists. There are hospitals that cater especially to sick cats and kennels or boarding places for cats—some are called "pussytels" or "cathotels." One woman in Australia who maintains a home away from home for cats whose owners are vacationing even prints a special daily menu for her distinguished temporary residents. Owners are advised to choose a cat's menus before leaving it for his, and their, holiday. The real menus of "pussytels" are careful, well-balanced lists of cats' favorite foods—fish, liver and other meats, milk, cat biscuits, and vitamins, and perhaps a bit of mouse or poultry. But it is easy to let the imagination wander and think of a cat's dream menu.

The poet Graham R. Thomson expressed very aptly the qualities which make the cat a perfect pet and suggests its very special appeal to human beings:

The Fireside Sphinx

by Graham R. Thomson

Half loving-kindliness and half disdain,
Thou comest to my call serenely suave,
With humming speech and gracious gestures grave,
In salutation courtly and urbane:

Yet must I humble me thy grace to gain—
For wiles may win thee, but no arts enslave,
And nowhere gladly thou abidest save
Where naught disturbs the concord of thy reign.

Sphinx of my quiet hearth! who deignst to dwell
Friend of my toil, companion of mine ease,
Thine is the lore of Ra and Rameses;
That men forget dost thou remember well,
Beholden still in blinking reveries,
With sombre sea-green gaze inscrutable.

The cat fancy grows continually larger and the cat population expands as well; in fact, it expands much more quickly than does the dog population. Cat popularity is increasing all the time—especially that of purebred animals such as Persians, Siamese, and Burmese. Men and women gain great pleasure from the companionship of the cat—its independence and its friendliness to those whom it likes make it a fascinating pet. The world is really divided into two parts: dog people and cat people. There are some men and women who are equally fond of dogs and cats, but they are few. One very famous man who loved both was Sir Winston Churchill. He had many favorite dogs, but he also had a pet cat that spent most of its time with the great statesman. The cat was a marmalade-colored pet, and it became famous in its own right because it accompanied Churchill to the cabinet meetings in England during World War II. While wartime matters of the utmost urgency were being debated and decided upon, the marmalade cat sat calmly on the floor washing her face with her paws.

There are famous people in all professions who are cat people. Among them are Picasso, ballerina Dame Margot Fonteyn, actor James Mason, playwright Noel Coward, novelists Truman Capote and Paul Gallico, poet and scholar Robert Graves, actresses Ursula Andress and Claudia Cardinale, and actress and singer Eartha Kitt, to name only a few. Famous people of the past who were cat lovers include Florence Nightingale, who never traveled without a cat in her declining years and who at one time kept over sixty cats, the painters Thomas Gainsborough and Sir Joshua Reynolds, and even Abraham Lincoln.

A cat who became famous shortly after the late President John F. Kennedy took office was Tom Kitten, the pet of Caroline Kennedy. Tom's life story was recounted in many papers throughout the states, not only because he was Caroline's pet but because he was the first White House cat since 1906, when President Theodore Roosevelt kept Slippers, a pretty gray, six-toed cat. Tom Kitten grew up at the Kennedy's Georgetown house and then moved into the White House on the blustery, snowy day after President Kennedy's Inauguration. The Washington *Daily News* later reported that it felt that Tom didn't enjoy living in the White House very much, and they quoted him as saying that there was "too much privacy and not enough cats around." Unfortunately, life soon grew to be too hectic for Tom at the White House—probably a result of too many diplomats, presidential assistants, and congressional dignitaries who tried to curry favor with him—and he moved from Washington, D. C., to Alexandria, Virginia, to stay with Mrs. Kennedy's personal secretary. He died in Alexandria of cirrhosis of the liver. In his obituary of August 22, 1962, the Alexandria *Gazette* commented favorably on his short stay at the nation's foremost residence: "Unlike many humans in the same position, he never wrote his memoirs of his days in the White House and never discussed them for quotation, though he was privy to many official secrets." There is a chance, of course, that he did leave a few paw prints on state documents and that these may be decoded at some later date so that history will have the benefit of Tom Kitten's opinion of the first one hundred days of the Kennedy Administration.

Another famous little cat whose adventures were thrilling is the kitten who climbed the Matterhorn—a fierce and icy peak in Switzerland that every mountain climber dreams of conquering. This kitten is one of the most heroic, courageous, and determined felines of the twentieth century.

Kitten's Escape

From *The Times,* London, 7th September 1950, *from our correspondent*

GENEVA, SEPTEMBER 6. A new conquest of the Matterhorn, this time by a 10-month-old black and white kitten, is reported from the Hotel Belvedere (10,820 ft.), on the Hornli Ridge—the starting point for alpinists attempting to climb the mountain.

The kitten, accustomed to watch from the hotel home the dawn departure of climbers, decided one morning to follow in their footsteps. He was soon left behind, but after a long and lonely climb reached the Solway hut (12,556 ft.). The next day he climbed still higher, and when night fell bivouacked in a *couloir* above the shoulder.

The next morning he was seen by a group of climbers, who passed him by, convinced that his climbing skill, if not his spirit, would be defeated by the difficult Ropes, Slabs and the Roof. They were wrong, and hours later the cat, miauling and tail up, reached the summit (14,780 ft.), where the incredulous climbing party rewarded him with a share in their meal.

The guide, who was leading his party down the Italian side of the Matterhorn, did not want to abandon the kitten on the top of the mountain, and as cats climb up much more easily than they climb down, the guide took him in his rucksack, brought him down to the Rifugio Principe Amedeo di Savoia (12,763 ft.), and left him there until some party returning to Zermatt could take him back. He is still there, happily fattening on mice whose lofty background and immunity hitherto from feline visits have made them easy prey. A season of easy hunting seems a small reward for the first cat to cross the Matterhorn.

The Alpine Journal in their issue of November, 1950, printed the following article about the mountain-climbing kitten:

New Conquest of the Matterhorn

by T. S. Blakeney

Mummery's well-known three categories of climbing difficulty—an inaccessible peak—the most difficult ascent in the Alps—an easy day for a lady—may stand in need of amendment, in view of the report (*The Times,* September 7, 1950) of an ascent of the Matterhorn by a 10-month-old kitten. Seeing the prowess of lady climbers nowadays, it might not be inappropriate to alter the third category to read "an easy climb for a cat."

Comte Alain de Suzannet has kindly sent us some particulars that correct the versions of the climb already in print. The kitten was 4 months old, not 10; and it followed a party led by Edmund Biner on August 18, but could not keep up and spent the night somewhere on the rocks. On August 19, Biner, with another party, saw the kitten on the mountainside and this time it kept pace with them, scaling the Moseley rocks to the right and left of the slabs and finding no great difficulty until the first rope was reached. From there up he (or "she," for the animal's sex seems unfathomable, changing from one to the other and back again in a bewildering manner) kept up with the party, but slightly to the right of the ropes, falling several times for short distances, but always stopping himself and never losing sight of the party. He reached the Swiss summit with the climbers and followed them to the Italian summit. As Biner was to descend the Italian ridge, he asked another guide, August Julen, to carry the kitten down to the Belvedere; but the animal refused and tried to stay with Biner and was eventually captured by a young guide from Breuil, named Pellisier, who took him down to the hotel above Breuil, the owner of which, Carrel, has promised to restore him to his mistress, Josephine Aufdenblatten, of the Belvedere. The stories of a night at the Solvay refuge and of fattening on mice, would appear to be inventions.

As a sporting venture, this episode will surely appeal to cat-lovers; to mountaineers it might well suggest that a good case has now been made out for the removal of all the ropes and chains that disfigure the Hörnli arête, since the kitten succeeded in making the climb without any of these superfluous aids.

Thurlow Craig, a newspaperman, recalled an experience of an old prospector friend of his which proved that "it doesn't pay to be clever with cats."

. . . The first time I visited his log cabin in the hills I noticed three little round holes in the bottom of his door and asked him what they were for.

"For my cats," he said. "I've got three."

"But why three holes?" I asked.

"Because when I say SCAT I mean SCAT," he replied calmly, and I roared with laughter at the idea of three tails vanishing through three holes simultaneously.

He went on to tell me about his patent chair. Every time he got up out of it a cat would hop up into the seat, and eventually he got fed up with picking cats out of it when he wanted to sit down.

Now the old-time prospector was many other things besides, a jack-of-all-trades. So this old boy got four hinges, a bolt, and made a lever that stuck up alongside, clear of one arm. He cut the seat in half, and the cushion too, nailing a half-cushion to each half-seat, hinging them each side to the frame of the chair. He installed the bolt underneath very securely, wired it strongly to the lever, and that was that.

If a cat got into that chair, all he had to do was to pull the lever, spring the trap, and the cat fell to earth with a bump. He would reset the contraption and seat himself comfortably on it. Although it took far more time to set, etcetera, than just picking a cat up and depositing it elsewhere, it was a most ingenious little invention.

Until one day the bolt sprung itself just as he sat down.

"There was I," he reminisced sadly, "stuck there like a damn fool as helpless as a baby. Couldn't move. If I hadn't had my bowie knife in my belt, the next visitor here would have found nothing but a skinny old skeleton sitting here. The laugh would have been on me. So when I rebuilt the chair, I made it old-style. The moral is, boy, it don't pay to be too scientific with cats."

The personality of each domestic cat is as different as that of each man or woman you meet. Carl Van Vechten wrote in *Tiger in the House:* "Each individual cat differs in as many ways as possible from each other individual cat. Any unprejudiced observer interested enough in cats to inspire their devotion will have found out for himself if he has ever become acquainted with several cats at one time." That may well be one of the reasons why people seldom tire of writing about the domestic cat and why there are always avid readers of anecdotes about cats in real life. No doubt, the life histories and the feats of common and uncommon cats will continue to be reported and commented upon for as long as men and cats remain on earth.

We do not know if cavemen and -women told each other stories about their domestic cats. We do know that Egyptians carved records of their domestic cats in stone hieroglyphs. From that day to this, humorous, sad, and admirable tales of cats have become part of man's daily life. The hundreds of fables, legends, short stories, novels, poems, and other fictional accounts of cats are more than equaled by the avalanche of anecdotes of domestic cats in everyday life.

One fascinating historical story which particularly appeals to all cat fanciers concerns a knight, Sir Henry Wyatt, who was imprisoned in the Tower of London near the end of the Wars of the Roses. Although Sir Henry was not mistreated in the Tower, he was not fed especially well either. One day a cat appeared on the window ledge of the room where he was imprisoned. In its mouth the cat was carrying a pigeon which it deposited on the sill before disappearing. The next day the cat appeared again, carrying another pigeon. Sir Henry persuaded his jail keepers to dress the birds for his meals, and the cat faithfully continued to provide the required birds. There is a painting which hangs today in the National Portrait Gallery in London which shows Wyatt and the cat with a pigeon in its mouth.

Today, newspapers, radio programs, and magazines continually carry articles and bulletins about the adventures of pet cats. These stories range from a cat that died of a broken heart when its owner went on vacation to the friendship of cats with turtles and mice and kangaroos and even to the cat friends and companions of famous and not-so-famous men and women.

There was one amusing letter to the editor printed in a newspaper in which a man wrote about his wife, who was such an extreme cat lover that she had practiced learning how to meow in response to cats' noises. After several years of her attempts to converse with the animals, she felt quite confident of her ability to communicate with them—at least she felt that she could establish a rapport with either familiar or strange cats when the occasion demanded. The letter writer did not mention whether or not the wife could understand exactly what the cats were saying or whether they understood her—there is some doubt on the latter point.

However, one warm summer evening, the man and his wife were strolling on a side street when they encountered an alley cat sitting on a fence. It meowed at them. The woman immediately responded with a meow, and after a few tentative exchanges between woman and cat, in varying tones, the conversation became louder, and the cat commenced howling. Obviously it had misunderstood the replies of the woman. The din of howling cat and meowing woman continued for several minutes, much to the husband's distress.

The cat grew even angrier and began spitting and hissing. The conversation was then stopped abruptly by a generous splashing of water from the sky. Looking up, the man realized that someone at an upper window of the building beside the fence had dumped a bucket of water on the "two fighting cats." Cat lovers sometimes have to pay a price for their familiarity with felines.

Anecdotes about cat adventures with and without humans abound, but a favorite topic with cat people is the acquiring of their very first cat. There are many memoirs of such incidents. Catherine Manley in *Your Cat and Mine* expressed the true cat person's feelings in her description of the experience of owning a kitten.

> A lovely thing it is to own one's own first kitten—soft and furry, curled comfortably before one's fireplace—or elusive with that hint of mystery, stalking the fallen leaves, lying in wait for birds and mice, peeping around the plants ready to surprise an unsuspecting mistress on her morning tour of the garden.
>
> All cats are lovely, whether born in catteries of the elite or in a humble kitchen. Over each we hold the power of life and death, a literally awful thought. Sometimes our friendship with them is so close that the veil between human and animal intelligence wears very thin—then one experiences the supreme thrill of keeping a cat, or perhaps allowing oneself to be owned by a cat.
>
> First of all we see, perhaps, one kitten amongst a litter that must be ours. That one and no other. Harden your heart and turn away if you are not prepared to sacrifice a

little of your time and freedom, for which you will be more richly rewarded than you deserve, then do not purchase that kitten. Let another, who is prepared to bestow the small price exacted, have the pleasure and joy it will bring.

It is not only the first cat that takes hold of the heart of a cat person. Once someone becomes a confirmed catophile, he can rarely resist the pleasure of owning a cat again. In *Mr. Cat,* George Freedly tells how he found and named his favorite Persian. All cat owners will recognize the symptoms of cat partisanship:

From Mr. Cat
by George Freedly

Catless and alone was my status in the summer of 1943. Deborah, my delightful Maltese who had been living with my parents in Winchester, had been run over by an automobile and killed. Guiltless of cat hairs was my Manhattan apartment and there wasn't a scratch or a scar on the upholstery. There were no imperious morning and nightly calls for attention and feeding. There was no cat in my life, save the memories of the many whom I had known and cherished since early childhood. In short, I wanted the soft affection, the alert mind, the beauty and homeliness of a cat about the house.

With this in mind, I called a friend then scouring the East Side pet shops on behalf of her husband who had suddenly developed a passion for small fish. I said I thought she *might* just add a glance about for a Persian kitten, one that might enliven and make my life savourable again.

Several days later, entering a Second Avenue emporium, Ruth heard vague noises of unmistakable kitten origin. After first conscientiously attending to her husband's affairs, Ruth made discreet inquiries and was promptly ushered to the back of the shop by the proprietor who produced four tiny balls of fur.

"I sensed at once," she told me later that evening, "that my search was over." I thanked her politely but cautiously and said that I would pass by in a day and take a look.

What a likely and hapless fool was I! You simply do not "take a look" at kittens when the need for cat companionship was as strong as mine. The next afternoon, on the fateful day of August 2, 1943, I entered the shop and asked if I too might see the kittens in residence. I too was led to the back, shown a small chicken coop and treacherously left to myself.

Four little Persians poured out, their bright eyes exploring the world. Four little Persians, but one only looked in my direction. I extended a tentative finger and two soft paws clung to it. There was a contented sound of purring, I suspect on both our parts.

Was there any decision to make? Besides, wasn't this the handsomest and certainly the most intelligent and friendliest? Besides, hadn't *he* chosen *me?* Indeed, the search was over.

My kitten's father was a handsome auburn to whom I was then presented. Father was most indifferent to the whole transaction and cared little about the fruit of his dalliance and obviously less about me. Mother and I never met, as she was kept at home with a lone kitten to keep her busy.

I carried my purchase off in a cardboard carton carefully punctured with air holes. As the proprietor bade me goodbye, I thought I spied a look of quiet satisfaction in his eye as though he had had no doubts of the charm of his kitten.

En route home in a taxi, the box let out some muffled cries. The cab came to a stop and my driver turned round with an accusing look which I hastened to allay.

"A cat!" he marveled, "You've got a cat in the box! Noises! I kept hearing noises and I looked everywhere and I couldn't see nothin'. A cat! I thought I was nuts."

As both of them had quietened down, the cab continued on its way and in a few minutes we swung off Madison Avenue west into 55th Street and stopped at *our* door. (Already I thought of it as his and mine). *Ours,* then, was a converted, five-story Victorian brownstone with a doorway hidden between two shop windows. Each floor of the house had but two apartments on it and ours was on the top.

As I entered the elevator, carefully balancing my carton, the neighbor with whom I shared the fifth floor joined me. When she heard the soft kitten mewing, she spoke in French rapidly (perhaps they don't speak in any other way) but I caught enough to learn that she adored cats and kittens and wanted to meet mine. Could she come in?

"Of course."

We entered my apartment together and when I had

loosened the cord, the top of the carton was pushed up by a little head. I set the box on the floor, tilting it a bit so that in a moment a very perky kitten emerged.

"May I pick him up?"

She could.

"Un chat. Un chat persien! Mademoiselle ou Monsieur?"

She determined by lifting its tail, despite indignant yowls at the other end.

She nodded: *"Monsieur Chat."*

And so that is how Mr. Cat came to be named.

The acquiring of a cat is the first order of business for cat fanciers. The next step is equally important: to secure the friendship of the animal. It is not enough merely to own a cat, the cat must want to belong to the owner or a great feeling of dissatisfaction will arise on both sides. Théophile Gautier, a great French author and cat fancier, explained the cat-human relationship and the lasting comfort it brings:

> To gain the friendship of a cat is a difficult thing. The cat is a philosophical, methodical, quiet animal, tenacious of his own habits, fond of order and cleanliness, and does not lightly confer his friendship. If you are worthy of his affection, a cat will be your friend but never your slave. He keeps his free will though he loves, and will not do for you what he thinks unreasonable; but if he once gives himself to you, it is with absolute confidence and fidelity of affection. He makes himself the companion of your hours of solitude, melancholy and toil. He will remain for whole evenings on your knee, uttering a contented purr, happy to

be with you. Put him down and he will jump up again with a sort of cooing sound like a gentle reproach; and sometimes he will sit upon the carpet in front of you looking at you with eyes so melting, so caressing and so human, that they almost frighten you, for it is impossible to believe that a soul is not there.

In addition to all the stories and anecdotes about cats, there are many products for sale which use the cat as their advertising symbol—a symbol guaranteed to appeal to all the cat fanciers. A well-known wallpaper manufacturing firm says their wall coverings have as many lives as "your own pet cat"; a photocopying company advertises that they are just like "copy cats"; carpets and blankets are "soft as a kitten"; car motors "purr" like a kitten—the list is endless.

The use of the advertising cat symbol caused a continual outpouring of articles about a famous real-life cat named Arthur, who lived in England. He ate a special brand of cat food with his paws on television advertisements. Poor Arthur became a pawn in a court case in February, 1968, between the man who claimed to be his owner and the cat-food firm which put out the ads Arthur appeared in. The cat-food firm said that they paid for Arthur and that they owned him. Arthur was hidden and the man who claimed to be his owner announced that he had handed the cat over to the Russian Embassy for "political asylum." But then the Russians would not admit that they knew of Arthur's whereabouts. Perhaps they had never been given him, or perhaps they weren't used to giving asylum to British cats. The case of ownership of Arthur went to the courts for decision, and the cat-food firm won. Arthur is certainly the most famous real cat in Britain today. He has even been the subject of poetry:

Arthur: The Teevee Cat (after Eliot)

by Angela Milne

A PRACTICAL Cat can dance at night,
Or rule a railway station;
But a Teevee Cat of purest white,
He is the real sensation.
Better than Jellicles full of fun,
Or Old Deuteronomy out in the sun,
Or Gus, Macavity, anyone,
Is Arthur, pride of the nation!

For a cat who eats from a tin with his paw,
As the cameras roll, is fabulous,
And a cat involved in a court of law
May fairly be called fantabulous;
But a snow-white cat who can do all that
And disappear from a Finchley flat
And be linked with a Mystery Diplomat—
I tell you, he's more than a Practical Cat,
He's a Cat Publicitipabulous!

Arthur is just one example of a famous cat which cat lovers enjoy hearing or reading about. And this story is a good example of the fact that the real-life adventures of cats are often as fantastic as the adventures of humans.

THE CAT HOROSCOPE

Because so many humans enjoy living with cats, the animals have even had their horoscopes charted—according to the month of their birthdays—so that men and women can choose a cat with a personality which will be compatible. One young cat lover has written *The Cat Horoscope Book* which should enable any cat owner to understand his pet's personality better. A typical horoscope for cats, for example, reads:

> ARIES (March 21–April 20): The original cat on a hot tin roof, most active and ambitious of them all. From clean laundry to flower beds, he makes a (hollow) impression everywhere. Fond of wandering, and when at home liable to create his own obstacle course with no inhibitions about broken ornaments. Fond of fighting, impetuous at loving. *Best Owners* (only owners able to survive him): Sagittarius, Leo. [*Aries* is the sign of the ram.]

> TAURUS (April 21–May 20): So placid and imperturbable that humans can understand him. So far from flighty that even danger will not stir his lazy bones. Taurus is dependable—you can depend on him to be forever in your way.
> *Best Owners:* Capricorn, Virgo, Cancer. [*Taurus* is the sign of the bull.]

> GEMINI (May 21–June 20): Essentially the kitten-cat, that exaggeratedly playful pussy with the gift of eternal youth. So far as felines fret, Gemini frets. He desires change of

scene, balls of wool; is much in demand for TV commercials. Incorrigibly bossy.
Best Owners: Libra, Aquarius, but never Taurus. [*Gemini* is the sign of twins.]

CANCER (June 21–July 20): Inconstant as the moon, deceitful as women, emotional as a Foreign Secretary, he swings from the chandelier and meows piteously in the corner; nobody can understand this cat. Regards humans as furniture.
Best Owners: Pisces, Scorpio. [*Cancer* is the sign of the crab.]

LEO (July 21–August 21): Pretentious—like his sign—authoritative, domineering, and ostentatious. From kittenhood, goes through life with the look of one who has his nose immediately above the smell of a rotting mouse. No tabby can resist him.
Best Owners: Aries, Sagittarius, but never Capricorn. [*Leo* is the sign of the lion.]

VIRGO (August 22–September 22): Conscientious, dedicated, down-to-earth. So domesticated that if you leave the beds until teatime, he glowers in disapproval. Careful never to harm a growing petunia, fussy enough to demand fresh food. Choosy about friends.
Best Owners: Capricorn, Taurus. [*Virgo* is the sign of the Virgin.]

LIBRA (September 23–October 22): Remember copy cats? That's Libra—which is why he studies his owner to an

extent, learning his mannerisms, adopting his habits. He prefers to look at life from your lap, to breakfast off eggs and bacon.
Best Owners: Leo, but never Aries. [*Libra* is the sign of the scales or balance.]

SCORPIO (October 23–November 22): Hidden beneath his prettily patterned fur lurks enough power for a fleet of bulldozers. Nobody ever got the better of this cat. He sums you up from the start. A hospitable cat, usually at your expense; likely to expect you to maintain his mate.
Best Owners: Cancer, Pisces. [*Scorpio* is the sign of the scorpion.]

SAGITTARIUS (November 23–December 20): A dreamy cat with the speed of a horse but the brain of a bird. This unsettling combination usually makes him as uncomfortable as he makes you. Not good in town—a dilapidated castle or old manor keeps him happiest.
Best Owners: Sagittarius, Leo, but never Cancer. [*Sagittarius* is the sign of the archer.]

CAPRICORN (December 21–January 19): A serious cat, most aptly named Prudence; cool, deliberate, a calculating cat indeed. If he cannot improve his owners, then he seeks a new family. Quickly house-trained, but too flirty for a happy love life.
Best Owners: Virgo, Libra, Taurus. [*Capricorn* is the sign of the goat.]

AQUARIUS (January 20–February 18): Meddlesome moggie, keen to have a paw in everybody's business. Appears to be kleptomaniac, but only steals a neighbor's petticoat or next-door's strawberry plants because he heard you admire them. Fond of humans.
Best Owners: Libra, Gemini, Aquarius. [*Aquarius* is the sign of the water bearer.]

PISCES (February 19–March 20): A difficult cat, often gay and moody, friendly but uncommunicative at the same time. Easily placated with promises of "fish tomorrow." The ideal ship's cat or theatre cat, for he loves the sea as much as play-acting.
Best Owners: Cancer, Scorpio, but never Capricorn. [*Pisces* is the sign of two fish—one swimming upstream and one swimming downstream.]

CAT PROVERBS

Through Aesop's Fables we know many cat proverbs. But Aesop was not the only person who invented them. There are hundreds of them in as many languages, and it is nearly impossible to say exactly which proverb came from which country and at which time in history. This is so because almost every country on earth where cats live has many cat proverbs, often very much alike, with only a word or two changed. Certainly the ancient Chinese, Arabs, Indians, and Egyptians all had cat proverbs. These wise sayings have been remembered through the centuries right down to our own time; in addition to these very old proverbs, there are some which are brand new. Certainly new cat proverbs will be invented in the future.

Most of the proverbs about cats can be roughly divided into two broad categories: cautionary tales and character sayings. The cautionary proverbs carry a warning about cats in general or in specific circumstances. The character proverbs point out how the cat behaves or what its personality is like—and, by inference, how people often behave. In the proverb "If a cat can't reach the roast, it is fasting," there is an immediate parallel drawn with people who cannot get something they want very much and then profess that they didn't really want whatever it was anyway. Another example, "A borrowed cat catches no mice," reminds men that others rarely lend worthwhile things, and that it is wise to be wary of borrowing.

These two short lists of cat proverbs show the variety and the effectiveness of the two types of sayings. There are, of course, hundreds and hundreds of similar proverbs, and both cat lovers and cat haters will probably be able to add to the lists without more than a minute's thought.

Cautionary Proverbs

A cat pent up becomes a lion.
Never put the kit to watch your chickens.
The tongue of the cat is poison; the tongue of the dog cures.
The dog wakes three times to watch over his master; the cat wakes three times to strangle him.
The cat always leaves a mark on his friend.

Care killed the cat.

Curiosity killed the cat; satisfaction brought it back.

He that denies the cat skimmed milk must give the rat cream.

God gave man the cat in order that he might have the pleasure of caressing the tiger.

It's the cornered cat who spits.

Beware the tiger that lurks in every cat.

Beware the cat in May.

A cat is a lion in a jungle of bushes.

There is no kitten too little to scratch.

Character Proverbs

The cat loves fish, but does not wish to wet its feet.

Never was cat or dog drowned that could see the shore.

To please himself only, the cat purrs.

An old cat knows fresh milk.

A gloved cat was never a good hunter.

A lame cat is better than a swift horse when rats are about.

The cat and dog may kiss, but are none the better friends.

The cat does not catch mice for God.

The cat makes sure whose chin it licks.

A cat is a cat.

A cat bitten once by a snake dreads even rope.

The cat who scratches, scratches for himself.

Old cats mean young mice; or, bashful cats, proud mice.

"The cat who miaous, hunts the less." Cervantes.

When the cat's away the mice will play.

"What's virtue in a man, can't be vice in a cat!" Mary Mapes Dodge.

"A cat will be your friend, but never your slave." Théophile Gautier.

CAT PHRASES

Dame Trot and her cat
Sat down for a chat;
The Dame sat on this side
And puss sat on that.

Puss, says the Dame,
Can you catch a rat,
Or a mouse in the dark?
Purr, says the cat.

From a very young age, most people are familiar with cat rhymes, but there is yet another part of cat lore that everyone knows—the many phrases and expressions derived from the word "cat." A dictionary could be made up of these words. Some of them are very old and their origin is lost to man's memory; the sources for others are easily recognizable. Here are a few of the most popular:

The name *cat* itself is often used to describe a woman. Perhaps this comes from the superstition that cats are two-faced and often false, and a man who has been spurned by a woman feels that she is being false, or catlike. Women are often by nature more languid than men, as cats are more languid than other animals, whereas man and dog are more active.

When a woman is gossiping about a friend she is said to be acting *"catty"*. This may come from the fact that cats can be very affectionate to someone they like and then in an instant jump off the person's lap and either spit in his direction or stalk off.

The name for a cat who is a companion of a witch is a *familiar* or *cat familiar.* This name comes from the medieval belief that the Devil frequently took the form of a black cat on earth, and witches were supposed to be servants of the Devil. A black cat that followed such a "witch" was called her cat familiar.

To cat, used as a verb, means to get sick or to vomit. This is probably because cats lick themselves continually and sometimes get sick as a result of hair balls sticking in their throats and also because cats almost always immediately disgorge anything in the way of food that does not agree with them.

The statement *It's enough to make a cat laugh* is obviously meant to refer to something that is completely ridiculous, for who ever saw a cat do anything as undignified as laughing?

It's raining cats and dogs is one of the best known of all cat phrases and means, of course, that it is pouring with rain. The phrase's origin is unclear, but, if rain is pelting down it can hurt; and if dogs and cats were falling from the sky pelting a person, that would hurt, too.

To *see how the cat jumps* is to look to see "which way the wind is blowing." Politicians can be accused of this, because they often wait to see how the public feels about a certain issue before committing themselves to an opinion. The phrase is an observation of how cats really do behave, for a cat never jumps anywhere without first looking to see what is in the way.

If a friend is behaving like *a cat walking on eggs,* the friend is obviously tiptoeing around or is terribly uneasy about something. Cats always walk very carefully. Anyone can readily imagine what a cat would look like walking on top of eggs.

To let the cat out of the bag is to disclose a secret. In olden days, farmers going to market often put a cat in a bag to take to market to sell rather than a pig which was the item prospective buyers thought they were purchasing.

Anyone who *turns cat in the pan* is a traitor. The phrase may well be a phonetic English translation of the French phrase *tourner côté en peine* which means to change sides when one is in trouble. No one knows for sure.

A boy or girl who is grinning widely at a joke can be said to be *grinning like a Cheshire cat.* Lewis Carroll in his famous book, *Alice in Wonderland,* depicted a Cheshire cat who grinned and grinned, but Carroll was not being original. The phrase is an old folk saying.

Someone who has drunk too much liquor has probably *had enough to make a cat speak*—which would be highly unlikely—but Shakespeare used the phrase in his play *The Tempest.*

A thief who is a *cat burglar* creeps in and out without making a sound, just as a cat can creep silently, but the term may really refer way back to the days when pewter mugs called "cat and kittens" were kept in old English inns. If someone stole the pewter cat and kittens, he would have been a *cat burglar.*

A *cat call* is a harsh whistle which audiences in movie

houses and theaters use sometimes to show that they think the picture or play is terrible. This is an obvious phrase, since the call of a cat on a backyard fence is horrible and usually precedes a fight with an enemy.

To play cat and mouse is a phrase which suggests that one person has another in his power in exactly the same way as a cat plays with a defenseless mouse.

Cat-eyed is an ancient description of someone who can see especially well. Even the Egyptians were aware that the cat could see very well in dim light, although a cat cannot see in absolute darkness.

A *cattail* is a long spikelike plant which grows in marshes; its flowers are soft, fuzzy, and brown and resemble a cat's tail. A *pussy willow* is another marsh plant which has small fuzzy gray flowers that feel like a kitten's fur.

Cat-lap is a name for a soft drink which is used in a derogatory way: "He's only old enough to drink cat-lap" would mean that someone was not legally old enough to drink hard liquor.

Cat's eye is a semiprecious stone such as quartz or chrysoberyl which has a changing appearance and which glows—very like the appearance of a real cat's eye.

If you like to take a *catnap* now and again, it means that you are probably able to lie down and go to sleep in a minute wherever you are, just as a cat can curl up anywhere and sleep lightly for a short while.

The *cat-o'-nine-tails* was a whip used to punish sailors on ships—sailors often shortened the name to *the cat.* The name of the whip with nine lashes may very well be a reference to the superstition that cats have nine lives.

A man who *lives under the cat's foot* is henpecked; he lives in the same way that a mouse lives.

Sailors call a light breeze which ripples the sea in very calm weather *a cat's paw*. The breeze touches the water in exactly the same way that a cat pats at water.

In the early 1900's and especially during the roaring twenties anything that was especially liked was called the *cat's pajamas* or the *cat's whiskers*. Whiskers are certainly something special, but whoever heard of pajamas for a cat? Maybe that is why the object so called was special. Flappers of the twenties also used the phrase the *cat's meow* to mean something special, and if they liked a handsome boy, he was "the cat's meow."

To walk *catty corner* or *kitty corner* is to walk at an angle rather than straight toward an object. Cats rarely approach anything head on; they prefer to sidle up to their target, rather than face an unknown and possibly dangerous object.

There are numerous other cat phrases, but they would fill a book by themselves. One of the most unusual stories which used cat phrases to make its point was written by Mark Twain. He wrote "A Cat-Tale" supposedly to amuse his little daughters and to teach them a lesson in manners, but the author's real purpose was to make fun of pompous adults. In "A Cat-Tale," Twain invented words with *cat* in them and gave new definitions to familiar words which included cat. Unfortunately, Twain got so carried away with his story and with the use of cat-words, that the story is difficult to read and is not nearly so funny as he intended it to be. Perhaps a few cat lovers might enjoy reading the story, but even that is doubtful. There is a field open, as a result of Twain's failure, for any cat lover who feels like writing a really funny story based on made-up cat-words.

But perhaps the cat-word story should be left to a new generation of cats to write. There is no doubt at all that at any time a new diary written by a cat will be published—even though the cat finds it necessary to dictate his memoirs to a willing human. Cats are more intelligent than people realize—why else would so many men and women sit down to write about and to explain their feelings about a domestic pet?

THE CAT IN LITERATURE

A proverb is a short, often very familiar saying which tells a well-known fact or expresses a truth which all men recognize as universal. One of the most famous of proverbs was used by Aesop in "But Who Is to Bell the Cat?" This short tale cleverly illustrates the familiar truth that it is easy to propose impossible solutions. Everyone, of course, knows that is so. But the truth of the saying is easier to understand and less painful to absorb because it is told in the form of a story.

Because cats are independent and, hence, more like man than other creatures, they often behave in ways that are similar to those of people. And these examples of behavior can be illustrated in stories which contain proverbs. The cat has long seemed to storytellers an excellent animal about which to invent stories which will teach the human race valuable lessons.

AESOP'S FABLES*

Aesop used the cat very effectively to teach human relations. And the fact that the fables of this man, who is thought to have been a Greek slave of African origin writing in the sixth century B.C., are still being rewritten, retold, modernized, and remembered is proof of their merit. Although Aesop's cat proverbs are not as well known as those which have a fox as a central character, the following selections demonstrate how the cat's personality lends itself to wise sayings.

Belling the Cat

Long ago, the mice held a general council to consider what measures they could take to outwit their common enemy, the Cat. Some said this, and some said that; but at last a young mouse got up and said he had a proposal to make, which he thought would meet the case. "You will all agree," said he, "that our chief danger consists in the sly and treacherous manner in which the enemy approaches us. Now, if we could receive some signal of her approach, we could easily escape from her. I venture, therefore, to propose that a small bell be procured, and attached by a ribbon round the neck of the Cat. By this means we should always know when she was about, and could easily retire while she was in the neighborhood."

This proposal met with general applause, until an old

* Fables quoted are from *The Fables of Aesop* as told anew by Joseph Jacobs.

mouse got up and said: "That is all very well, but who is to bell the Cat?" The mice looked at one another and nobody spoke. Then the old mouse said: "It is easy to propose impossible remedies."

The Fox and the Cat

A fox was boasting to a Cat of its clever devices for escaping its enemies. "I have a whole bag of tricks," he said, "which contains a hundred ways of escaping my enemies."

"I have only one," said the Cat; "but I can generally manage with that." Just at that moment they heard the cry of a pack of hounds coming towards them, and the Cat immediately scampered up a tree and hid herself in the boughs. "This is my plan," said the Cat. "What are you going to do?" The fox thought first of one way, then of another, and while he was debating the hounds came nearer and nearer, and at last the Fox in his confusion was caught up by the hounds and soon killed by the huntsmen. Miss Puss, who had been looking on, said: "Better one safe way than a hundred on which you cannot reckon."

The Cat Maiden

The gods were once disputing whether it was possible for a living being to change its nature. Jupiter said "Yes," but Venus said "No." So, to try the question, Jupiter turned a Cat into a Maiden, and gave her to a young man for wife.

The wedding was duly performed and the young couple sat down to the wedding feast. "See," said Jupiter to Venus, "how becomingly she behaves. Who could tell that yesterday she was but a Cat? Surely her nature is changed?"

"Wait a minute," replied Venus, and let loose a mouse into the room. No sooner did the bride see this than she jumped up from her seat and tried to pounce upon the mouse.

"Ah, you see," said Venus, "Nature will out."

THE CAT IN FOLKLORE

For thousands of years cat stories in the form of myths or legends or fables have been popular. Perhaps this is because men have often felt that the cat acted more like a human being than other creatures. Or perhaps the stories arose because men couldn't quite understand why a cat could be aloof sometimes and affectionate at other times. Because a cat is so independent in nature, men have assumed that it is more intelligent than other animals; and because a cat can be very disdainful, a trait no other animal really possesses, men have assumed that it felt superior to themselves and other animals. It may be the trait of looking upon people's actions while seeming neither to approve nor disapprove that has fascinated men most and led them to describe and portray cats in stories as wise, all-knowing, magical, and superior.

But there is another side to the story. As often as the cat has been depicted as wise and superior, it has also been shown to be greedy, mean, or despicable. The traits of independence and superiority which a cat exhibits have sometimes found favor with man, and at other times incurred his wrath or at least his dislike.

While the early Egyptians liked and worshiped cats, other peoples were not disposed to feel kindly toward the animal. This dislike shows in many of the early fables and legends about cats.

The beast fables of Bidpai recorded in *The Panchatantra,* written about three hundred years before the birth of Jesus, show the cat to be a greedy, ambitious, or devious creature. Obviously, the people of India did not have as high a regard for cats as did the Egyptians.

In his fables, Aesop frequently depicted cats at odds with mice. The mice were almost always the heroes, and the cats were sneaky or mean or greedy. There were many other Greeks besides Aesop who wrote bestiaries, or animal fables, but they did not give the cat a prominent role in their tales. Neither did the Christian bestiary writers of the Middle Ages. Evidently, Christians did not find the cat a worthy animal, or in their zeal to erase all memory of pagan religions they deliberately excluded the cat, which had been featured in such non-Christian rituals.

There is no mention of the cat in the Bible except for a few fleeting mentions of it in the Apocryphal Book of Baruch. There is nothing long enough to be considered a story or even a fable or proverb.

The Jews either did not know the domestic cat or did not care for it. There is no mention of the animal in the *Torah;* the word "Chatul" does appear in the *Talmud,* but the Judeo-Aramaic word "chatul" probably refers to a pole-cat rather than a pet cat.

There were early legends about cats which the Chinese,

Japanese, and other Oriental peoples told. The Japanese "vampire cat" was a scary specter which tried to kill people in the nighttime and which was often shown in delicately drawn pictures.

In the seventeenth century, the Western world began to show more interest in cats, and fables and legends concerning them became more widely popular. La Fontaine, a Frenchman who is famous for adopting legends and old stories which we know as our favorite fairy tales, worked with Aesop's fables and made popular some longer stories taken from the Greek's work. Charles Perrault, another Frenchman who lived in the seventeenth century, wrote the story called "Puss-in-Boots," which is beloved by younger children. Puss is a handsome, swashbuckling hero and one of the most attractive cats in fiction.

The German brothers, Jacob and Wilhelm Grimm, also retold many cat fables which were based upon folk stories they had collected.

One of the most famous of all cat fables is the French story "The White Cat." The tale concerns a beautiful cat who had been changed into a princess but who cannot hide her real nature from her suitor and at a crucial moment dashes away to chase a rat which has appeared. This part fairy tale, part legend is almost an exact lengthened retelling of one of Aesop's proverbs about the cat.

Whether the stories are famous or not, people all over the world have recounted legends about cats. Russia, Spain, Italy, Germany, Finland, France, Scotland, Egypt, Britain, America, and many other countries all have their cat stories.

One of the most charming cat-folk-legends originated long ago in Poland. The story is about the pussy-willow plant which grows on riverbanks in spring. A beautiful gray mother cat had a litter of kittens one springtime. All of them looked exactly like tiny replicas of her. The farmer to whom the adult cat belonged would not tolerate having so many cats about to feed, and so he took the kittens to a nearby river and tossed them into the water. The mother cat wept so loudly and so pitifully on the riverbank that the willows growing there consulted among themselves and decided to stretch their long slender stalks toward the water to help. The kittens were able to grasp the stalks with their small claws and were thus saved from drowning. And each spring, in memory of the kindness of those plants, pussy willows grow soft gray, furry buds, which feel like the fur of newborn kits.

Another very old legend is told by the Arabs about Muezza, the favorite cat of Mohammed. The cat was asleep on the sleeve of Mohammed's robe, and the prophet had to go away. He cut off the sleeve and allowed the cat to continue its nap. When the prophet returned, the cat bowed before him in grateful thanks. Then the Moslem leader stroked the creature's back three times and thus conferred upon the cat and all its descendants the ability always to fall upon its feet.

"Why Cat Is Indoors and Dog Outside in the Cold" is an old folktale from Ireland. The story is supposed to explain why dogs always bark at strangers and beggars, but it is easy to see that, like other tales and legends about cats, the story shows that cats have always been thought to be cleverer than other domestic animals. Just as in Kipling's story about the cat who walked alone, the cat here manages to provide food and comfort for himself by being just a little smarter and shrewder than either man or dog.

Why Cat Is Indoors and Dog Outside in the Cold

retold by Sean O'Sullivan

Long ago the dog used to be out in the wet and the cold, while the cat remained inside near the fire.

One day, when he was "drowned wet," the dog said to the cat, "You have a comfortable place, but you won't have it any longer. I'm going to find out whether I have to be outside every wet day, while you are inside."

The man of the house overheard the argument between the two and thought that it would be right to settle the matter.

"Tomorrow," said he, "I will start a race between ye five miles from the house, and whichever of ye comes into the house first will have the right to stay inside from then on. The other can look after the place outside."

Next day, the two got themselves ready for the race. As they ran toward the house, the dog was a half mile ahead of the cat. Then he met a beggarman. When the beggarman saw the dog running toward him with his mouth open, he thought he was running to bite him. He had a stick in his hand, and he struck the dog as he ran by. The dog was hurt and started to bark at the beggarman and tried to bite him for satisfaction.

Meanwhile the cat ran toward the house, and she was licking herself near the fire and resting after the race when the dog arrived.

"Now," said the cat when the dog ran in, "the race is won, and I have the inside of the house for evermore."

"Why the Siamese Cat Has a Kink in Her Tail" is an ancient legend from Siam, now Thailand. Siamese cats were known for their special and distinctive appearance—crossed blue eyes, dark-brown mask and ears and paws, and a tail which had a slight bend about an inch from the tip. Today, cat breeders feel that the crossed eyes and kink in the tail are flaws, and the cats are carefully bred to remove the characteristics which distinguished this aristocratic breed. It seems only natural that a folktale explaining how the distinctive markings first appeared would circulate among people who held the Siamese in great esteem.

Why the Siamese Cat Has a Kink in Her Tail

Once long ago, in the ancient kingdom of Siam, two very beautiful and proud cats lived in a temple guarding the treasures upon the altar night and day. As it happened, and no one, not even the temple priests, knew how, a royal goblet was discovered to be missing.

The Chief Priest of the temple was very distressed, for the goblet was valuable, and so he sent the two cats, who were called Tien and Chula, into the jungle to hunt for the precious treasure. For many days they traveled, deep into the heart of the steaming jungle, and at last when they arrived at the side of a stream, footsore and weary, they found the goblet, hidden under the root of a huge tree.

The cats conferred with one another and decided that Chula should remain to guard the treasure, while Tien journeyed back to the temple to tell the Chief Priest of their discovery. And so he set out, leaving his faithful mate to keep watch lest the treasure be stolen again.

After he had departed, Chula sat down beside the goblet. Day after day she waited, never taking her beautiful eyes, which were as blue as the sky on a midsummer's day, off the goblet. As the days wore on and Chula continued to stare at the goblet, her eyes gradually grew weary and she began to squint. At last weariness overcame her and she was forced to lie down to sleep. But before she closed her eyes, she carefully wrapped her tail round the stem of the goblet so that she would awaken if anyone chanced to try to steal it.

At last Tien returned to the heart of the jungle where Chula waited. To his delight and surprise he found that he was the father of five newly born kittens. Although the little ones were playing around their mother, she still lay with her tail wrapped firmly about the goblet, guarding the treasure. When she unwrapped her tail, lo and behold! there was a kink in its end, and when she gazed up happily at her mate, her lovely blue eyes still squinted. And each of the kittens had a tiny kink in the end of its tail and a squint in its eyes.

And from that day to this, in memory of Chula who guarded the precious royal goblet so faithfully, all Siamese cats have a kink in their tail and a squint in their beautiful blue eyes.

The story "How Cats Came to Purr" imitates successfully, in both language and feeling, very ancient legends, although it was written in the 1920's. It is similar to old beast tales, for there is a very subtle moral to the story; and in the end the clever cat is outwitted and punished for his lies, and a curse is put on all his descendants. The cat has a personality of infinite variety which has fascinated tellers of fables and legends for centuries. When man is journeying to galaxies far beyond the Milky Way in future years, it is more than likely that writers will still be inventing and imagining fables and legends to explain cat characteristics or to amuse and instruct readers by the cat's good or bad example.

How Cats Came to Purr

by John Bennett

A boy having a pet cat which he wished to feed, said to her, "Come, cat, drink this dish of cream; it will keep your fur soft as silk, and make you purr like a coffee-mill."

He had no sooner said this than the cat, with a great glare of her green eyes, bristled her tail like a gun-swab, and went over the back fence, head-first—pop!—as mad as a wet hen.

And this is how she came to do so:

The story is an old one—very, very old. It may be Persian; it may be not: that is of very little moment. It is so old that if all the nine lives of all the cats that have ever lived in the world were set up together in a line, the other end of it would just reach back to the time when this occurred.

And this is the story:

Many, many years ago, in a country which was quite as far from anywhere else as the entire distance thither and back, there was a huge cat that ground the coffee in the king's kitchen, and otherwise assisted with the meals.

This cat was, in truth, the actual and very father of all subsequent cats, and his name was Sooty Will, for his hair was as black as a night in a coal-hole. He was ninety years old, and his moustaches were like whisk-brooms. But the most singular thing about him was that in all his life he had never once purred nor humped up his back, although his master often stroked him. The fact was that he never had learned to purr, nor had any reason, so far as he knew, for humping up his back. And being the father of all cats, there was no one to tell him how. It remained for him to acquire a reason, and from his example to devise a habit which cats have followed from that time forth, and no doubt will forever follow.

The king of the country had long been at war with one of his neighbors; but one morning he sent back a messenger to say that he had beaten his foeman at last, and that he was coming home for an early breakfast as hungry as three bears. "Have batter-cake and coffee," he directed, "hot and plenty of 'em!"

At that the turnspits capered and yelped with glee, for batter-cakes and coffee are not cooked upon spits, and so they were free to sally forth into the city streets and watch the king's home-coming in a grand parade. But the cat sat down on his tail in the corner and looked cross. "Scat!" said he, with an angry caterwaul. "It is not fair that you should go and that I should not."

"Oh, yes, it is," said the gleeful turnspit. "Turn and turn about is fair play: you saw the rat that was killed in the parlor."

"Turn about fair play, indeed!" cried the cat. "Then all of you get to your spits; I am sure that is turn about!"

"Nay," said the turnspits, wagging their tails and laughing. "That is over and over again, which is not fair play. 'Tis the coffee-mill that is turn and turn about. So turn to your mill, Sooty Will; we are off to see the king!"

With that they pranced out into the courtyard, turning handsprings, headsprings, and heel-springs as they went, and, after giving three hearty and vociferous cheers in a grand chorus at the bottom of the garden, went capering away for their holiday.

The cat spat at their vanishing heels, sat down on his tail in the chimney-corner, and was very glum indeed.

Just then the cook looked in from the pantry. "Hullo!" he said gruffly. "Come, hurry up the coffee!" That was the way he always gave his orders.

The black cat's whiskers bristled. He turned to the mill with a fierce frown, his long tail going to and fro like that of a tiger in its lair; for Sooty Will had a temper like hot gunpowder, that was apt to go off sizz, shizz, bang! and no one to save the pieces. Yet, at least while the cook was by, he turned the mill furiously, as if with a right goodwill.

Meantime, out in the city, a glorious day came on. The sun went buzzing up the pink-and-yellow sky with a sound like that of a walking-doll's works, or of a big Dutch clock behind a door; banners waved from the castled heights, and bugles sang from every tower; the city gates rang with the cheers of the enthusiastic crowd. Up from cellars, down from lofts, off workbenches, and out at the doors of their masters' shops, dodging the thwacks of their masters' straps, "pop-popping" like corks from the necks of so many bottles, came apprentices, shop-boys, knaves and scullions, crying: "God save the king! Hurrah! Hurrah! Masters and work may go to Rome; our tasks shall wait on our own sweet wills; 'tis holiday when the king comes home. God save the king! Hurrah!"

Then came the procession. There were first three regiments of trumpeters, all blowing different tunes; then fifteen regiments of mounted infantry on coal-black horses, forty squadrons of green-and-blue dragoons, and a thousand drummers and fifers in scarlet and blue and gold, making a thundering din with their rootle-te-tootle-te-tootle-te-rootle; and pretty well up to the front in the ranks was the king himself, bowing and smiling to the populace, with his hand on his breast; and after him the army, all in shining armor, just enough pounded to be picturesque, miles on miles of splendid men, all bearing the trophies of glorious war, and armed with lances, and bows and arrows, falchions, morgensterns, martels-de-fer, and other choice implements of justifiable homicide, and the reverse, such as hautboys, sackbuts and accordions and dudelsacks and Scotch bagpipes—a glorious sight!

And, as has been said before, the city gates rang with the cheers of the crowd, crimson banners waved over the city's pinnacled summits, and bugles blew, trumpets brayed, and drums beat until it seemed that wild uproar and rich display had reached its high millennium.

The black cat turned the coffee-mill. "My oh! My oh!" he said. "It certainly is not fair that those bench-legged turnspits with feet like so much leather should see the king marching home in his glory, while I, who go shod, as it were, in velvet, should hear only the sound through the scullery windows. It is not fair. It is no doubt true that 'The cat may mew, and the dog shall have his day,' but I have as much right to my day as he; and has it not been said from immemorial time that 'A cat may look at a king'? Indeed, it has, quite as much as that the dog may have his day. I will not stand it; it is not fair. A cat may look at a king; and if any cat may look at a king, why, I am the cat who may. There are no other cats in the world; I am the only one. Poh! the cook may shout till his breath gives out, he cannot frighten me; for once I am going to have my fling!"

So he forthwith swallowed the coffee-mill, box, handle, drawer-knobs, coffee-well, and all, and was off to see the king.

So far, so good. But, ah! the sad and undeniable truth, that brightest joys too soon must end! Triumphs cannot last forever, even in a land of legends. There comes a reckoning.

When the procession was past and gone, as all processions pass and go, vanishing down the shores of forgetfulness; when barons, marquises, dukes, and dons were gone, with their pennants and banners; when the last lancers had gone prancing past and were lost to sight down the circuitous avenue, Sooty Will, with drooping tail, stood by the palace gate, dejected. He was sour and silent and glum. Indeed, who would not be, with a coffee-mill on his conscience? To own up to the entire truth, the cat was feeling decidedly unwell. When suddenly the cook popped his head in at the scullery entry, crying, "How now, how now, you vagabonds! The war is done, but the breakfast is not. Hurry up, scurry up, scamper and trot! The cakes are all cooked and are piping hot! Then why is the coffee so slow?"

The king was in the dining hall, in dressing gown and slippers, irately calling for his breakfast!

The shamefaced, guilty cat ran hastily down the scullery stairs and hid under the refrigerator, with such a deep inward sensation of remorse that he dared not look the kind cook in the face. It now really seemed to him as if everything had gone wrong with the world, especially his own insides. This anyone will readily believe who has ever swallowed a coffee-mill. He began to weep copiously.

The cook came into the kitchen. "Where is the coffee?" he said. Then, catching sight of the secluded cat, he stooped, crying, "Where is the coffee?"

The cat sobbed audibly. "Someone must have come into the kitchen while I ran out to look at the king!" he gasped, for there seemed to him no way out of the scrape but by telling a plausible untruth. "Someone must have come into the kitchen and stolen it!" And with that, choking upon the handle of the mill, which projected into his throat, he burst into inarticulate sobs.

The cook, who was, in truth, a very kind-hearted man, sought to reassure the poor cat.

"There; it is unfortunate, very; but do not weep; thieves thrive in kings' houses!" he said, and stooping, he began to stroke the drooping cat's back to show that he held the weeping creature blameless.

Sooty Will's heart leaped into his throat.

"Oh, oh!" he half gasped, "oh, oh! If he rubs his great hands down my back he will feel the corners of the coffee-mill through my ribs as sure as fate! Oh, oh! I am a gone cat!" And with that, in an agony of apprehension lest his guilt and his falsehood be thus presently detected, he humped up his back as high in the air as he could, so that the corners of the mill might not make bumps in his sides and that the mill might thus remain undiscovered.

But, alas! he forgot that coffee-mills turn. As he humped up his back to cover his guilt, the coffee-mill inside rolled over, and, as it rolled, began to grind—rr-rr-rr-rr-rr-rr-rr-rr-rr-rr!

"Oh, oh! You have swallowed the mill!" cried the cook.

"No, no," cried the cat, "I was only thinking aloud."

At that out stepped the Genius that lived under the great ovens, and, with his finger pointed at the cat, said in a frightful voice, husky with wood-ashes: "Miserable and pusillanimous beast! By telling a falsehood to cover a wrong you have only made bad matters worse. For betraying man's kindness to cover your shame, a curse shall be upon you and all your kind until the end of the world. Whenever men stroke you in kindness, remembrance of your guilt shall make you hump up your back with shame, as you did to avoid being found out. And in order that the reason for this curse shall never be forgotten, whenever man is kind to a cat a sound of the grinding of a coffee-mill inside shall perpetually remind him of your guilt and shame!"

With that the Genius vanished in a cloud of smoke.

And it was even as he said. From that day Sooty Will could never abide having his back stroked without humping it up to conceal the mill within him; and never did he hump up his back but the coffee-mill began slowly to grind, rr-rr-rr-rr! inside him; so that, even in the prime of life, before his declining days had come, being seized upon by a great remorse for these which might never be amended, he retired to a home for aged and reputable cats, and there, so far as the records reveal, lived the remainder of his days in charity and repentance.

But the curse has come down even to the present day—as the Genius that lived under the great ovens said—and still maintains, though cats have probably forgotten the facts, and so, when stroked, hump up their backs and purr as if these actions were a matter of pride instead of being a blot upon their family record.

This short poem, written by an unknown author, supposedly explains why the Manx cats almost never have tails; sometimes they do have a short stump of a tail, but that is very rare. The Isle of Man, sometimes called "Mona," is located off the coast of England, and the people who live there are called Manxmen. The island is famous for its tailless cats.

How Did the Manx Cat Lose His Tail?

Noah sailing o'er the seas
Ran high and dry on Ararat.
His dog then made a spring and took
The tail from off a pussy cat.

Puss through the window quick did fly
And bravely through the waters swam,

Nor even stopped till high and dry
She landed on the Isle of Man.

This tailless puss earned Mona's thanks
And ever after was called Manx.

Another old legend in the form of an anonymous poem about the Manx cat and the Ark gives a slightly different version of why the breed has no tail: When the waters of the Flood had risen too high for safety and the Ark was ready to sail, the poor cat was late and as a result had an unfortunate accident.

Said the cat, and he was a Manx,
Oh, Captain Noah, wait!
I'll catch the mice to give you thanks
And pay for being late!
So the cat got in, but oh,
His tail was a bit too slow.

"The Devout Cat," or "The Cat's Judgment," is a very, very old story from a book of wise sayings and fables called *The Panchatantra.* This book was written by an ancient court scholar of India, or perhaps by several men. We do not know for sure because the author's name, Bidpai, was a title given to a learned man of the time. The story has come to us through an Arabic retelling of the lost work in Sanskrit, called *The Fables of Bidpai.* This type of fable, called a beast fable, was written to teach men through the example of animal behavior how to live better lives. In that respect, it is similar to animal proverbs.

The Cat's Judgment or the Devout Cat

Long ago, when animals spoke freely with one another and had but little trouble understanding the language of creatures not of their own kind, a quail built a nest in a bush near a river. She lived there happily for some time and raised a small family. One day, when her chicks had grown large enough to go out into the world, the mother quail guided them away, leaving her nest. She was absent for some time and the nest remained quite empty.

As it happened, a proud hare moved into the neighborhood near the river and finding the nest abandoned and very much to his liking, he decided to settle there. He lived happily for many months in the nest. The river provided him with clear, fresh water and on its bank sprouted tender shoots which gave him a wonderful meal whenever he was inclined to be hungry.

Several months had passed, when the quail suddenly returned to her former home. She was angry at finding her carefully built nest occupied.

"Go away, thief!" she screamed, flapping her wings furiously. "Go away! That is my nest, which I spent many laborious hours constructing. Out! Out! Out!"

But the hare did not wish to leave, and he did not feel at all like a thief, for the nest had long been empty.

"*Your* nest?" he inquired with a flick of one ear. "It was abandoned when I found it. Finder's are keeper's by law. It is *my* nest, now."

"Abandoned or not when you found it, *I* built the nest and by right it should belong to me," the quail cried.

"You may very well have built it," the hare said, "but I kept it from decaying. It was in a terrible state and I worked very hard to repair the damage. *Now, it is my home.*"

The quail flew at the hare ready to peck him and screamed, "I have witnesses to prove it is mine."

The hare was unmoved, but he shifted in order to be able to kick if he were attacked. "I have witnesses, too," he replied.

At that moment a bushy-tailed squirrel rushed by the nest, and hearing the furious squabbling he stopped to listen.

"Friends," he called in a trembling voice, "perhaps the good and devout hermit could judge who owns the nest. It is said that he is wise and spends his days all alone contemplating the goodness of nature and the wiseness of God."

"The hermit?" asked the hare and the quail together. Both were very surprised. "Who is this devout hermit?"

"Oh, the great cat who lives in the cave not far from the river's beginning," the squirrel replied, growing more bold.

"The great cat!" said the quail.

"The cat!" said the hare.

"Oh, no"—the pair shook their heads—"he wouldn't be a good judge."

"And besides," the quail added, "that would be very dangerous for us."

"Oh, he is reputed to be both wise and good," the squirrel said, "and I hear he never eats anyone, especially not those who seek his advice and wise counsel."

"Well . . ." pondered the quail.

"What a good idea," said the hare, "let us go and ask the great cat to judge whom the nest belongs to."

"Yes," the quail agreed, "then the problem can be settled amicably."

And they set out immediately for the place where the river began.

When the cat saw the quail and the hare approaching, being as wise as his reputation, he guessed that they must be coming to settle the question of the nest's ownership, for news traveled quickly beside the river. He stretched out full length on the floor of the cave, dropped his head onto his great paws, curled his tail around his body, and narrowed his eyes to thin slits. He looked as thoughtful and as serene as possible.

When the pair were still some distance from the entrance to the cave, the quail called out in a brave voice, "O, great and wise cat, forgive us for disturbing your thoughts, but we want to ask you the favor of settling a quarrel."

"We have heard how wise and good and devout you are," the hare called out in a voice calculated to flatter the cat.

The great cat blinked his eyes and slowly put his right paw up to his ear. "You will have to come closer," he purred. "I see very few people and am growing hard of hearing, it seems."

The quail and the hare moved closer and repeated their previous words.

The cat shut both his eyes and twitched his whiskers in an effort to hear them.

"Nearer, nearer, you'll have to come nearer. I really am going quite deaf," he purred.

The quail and the hare moved even nearer and tried again to explain what they wanted.

"Tut! Tut!" the great cat said, turning his head to one side. "You'll have to come and speak right into my ear or else I shall never understand what it is you require. Speak more loudly, please."

The quail and the hare were becoming quite desperate, so, losing all caution, they rushed right up to the cat and, one on each side, they began to shout into the great cat's ears about the quarrel over the nest.

With a leap and a swish of his tail, the cat stunned them both into insensibility and then proceeded with great relish to eat up his visitors.

And that is how the devout cat settled the quarrel between the quail and the hare.

Perhaps, my friends, the quail and the hare were too willing to trust the good reputation of an animal cleverer than they.

The following story of how a cat got revenge for his friend's death has been told for years on the Island of Corsica, in the Mediterranean Sea. Although it does not have an obvious moral, as most of Aesop's fables do, it is easy to see that the native Corsicans who told the story believed that a cat could be a good animal, but that men and other animals were evil or uncaring. The kitten's death is revenged, not because the cat actually set out to punish those responsible, but because fate caused a series of accidents which resulted in the revenge. The themes of revenge and of fate taking a hand in daily events have always been popular with Italian country people, and it seems logical that they should tell a story of revenge in the form of an animal fable.

How the Tom Cat Got Revenge for the Kitten's Death

Once upon a time and long ago, a huge Tom cat and a tiny kitten lived together in a handsome cottage near a forest. They were the greatest of friends and shared the work of keeping the house in order. They shared, too, whatever food came their way. If the huge Tom cat caught a huge rat, he divided the meat so that the kitten would have a small portion; and if the kitten caught a mouse, she always invited the Tom to have a larger portion. Both the Tom cat and the kitten shared a liking for a special treat: the sweet meat inside of nuts. Whenever one or the other came upon a single nut in the forest, they always shared, or if luck was especially good they shared a whole pile of nuts.

One day, as fortune would have it, the cat made a discovery and then said to the kitten: "It is time for our favorite treat. The squirrel has left a pile of hazelnuts in the loft. Let's go up and have a feast."

The kitten's eyes shone and she replied in a purring voice: "Oh yes, let's go have a feast."

So they both leapt up to the loft and prepared to enjoy the nuts.

"Wait, dear kitten," said the Tom, holding up a cautionary paw, for he was older and wiser and patient. "Be careful not to eat the shells in your haste. You could easily choke to death."

"Thank you for warning me," said the kitten, and she pounced on a nearby pile of hazelnuts and began gobbling them up as quickly as possible. The nuts were so delicious that she immediately forgot the Tom cat's words and swallowed a nut, shell and all.

"Oh! Help! I am choking to death," she gasped and coughed in a pitiful way.

The Tom cat spit out the nut he was chewing, rushed to her side and began to thump her on the back with his paw, but the nut remained lodged in the kitten's throat.

"I must get some butter to grease her throat or she will very soon die," Tom said.

So he leapt down to the cupboard to get some butter, but alas, the cupboard was locked.

"Oh, cupboard, cupboard, open up, please. I must get some butter to grease kitten's throat or she will very soon die," Tom said.

"Run to the locksmith and bring back a key," the cupboard replied in a creaky voice.

So Tom ran to the locksmith to bring back a key.

"Locksmith, locksmith, make me a key, please. I must have a key to open the cupboard to get some butter to grease kitten's throat or she will very soon die," Tom said.

"First run to the shopkeeper and get me some cheese," the locksmith said in a very firm voice.

So Tom ran to the shopkeeper to get some cheese.

"Oh, shopkeeper, shopkeeper, give me some cheese, please, to give to the locksmith who'll make me a key to open the cupboard to get some butter to grease kitten's throat or she will very soon die," Tom said.

"First run to the cow and get me some milk," the shopkeeper said in a very rough voice.

So Tom ran to the cow to ask her for milk.

"Cow, cow, give me some milk, please, to give to the shopkeeper to get some cheese to give to the locksmith who'll make me a key to open the cupboard to get some butter to grease kitten's throat or she will very soon die," Tom said.

"First run to the meadow to ask for some grass."

"Oh, meadow, meadow, give me some grass, please, to give to the cow to get milk for the shopkeeper who'll give me some cheese for the locksmith who'll make me a key to open the cupboard to get some butter to grease kitten's throat or she will very soon die," Tom said.

"First ask the sky to give me rain," the meadow said in a whispery voice.

"Oh, sky, sky, give us rain, please, so the meadow will give me some grass for the cow who'll give me some milk for the shopkeeper who'll give me cheese for the locksmith who'll make me a key to open the cupboard to get some butter to grease kitten's throat or she will very soon die," Tom cried.

And the sky took pity on the poor Tom cat and rain began to fall on the meadow which gave grass for the cow who gave milk for the shopkeeper who gave cheese for the locksmith who made a key to open the cupboard. And Tom got the butter to grease kitten's throat, but when he leapt again up to the loft he found her lying on her back with her four paws in the air. She had soon choked to death on the hazelnut shell.

Tom wept and cursed and cried over the kitten. He

carried her down from the loft and buried her under a hazelnut tree and mournfully kept watch over her grave. In his sorrow he forgot to eat the nuts which fell and he stopped catching rats. So the rats multiplied and they gnawed through the cupboard and through all the other cupboards in the village and the locksmith had no work making keys and he died of hunger so there was no one to buy cheese and the shopkeeper was ruined and there was no one to want milk and the cow was sent to be slaughtered so the meadow was soon full of weeds. The sky sent more rain and soon a little river formed and rushed by the hazelnut tree where the kitten was buried and Tom followed the river to another village and all behind him was left in ruins. And that is the story of how the Tom cat got revenge for the death of the kitten.

NO DOUBT CATS TALK AND REASON

Famous writers—almost too many to name—have loved cats and have written about them. Some have acknowledged that their cats provided them with inspiration for books and poems. A few writers have even gone so far as to state that they were sure their cats could write books themselves, if only the animals were able to hold a pen or typewrite in English or French or German or some other language that humans could understand.

It seems that writers have credited cats with an extraordinary amount of intelligence and certainly with more common sense than human beings. Izaak Walton, the great English author of *The Compleat Angler,* talks in his book about another famous writer who loved cats, Montaigne. That

French essayist and philosopher who lived in the sixteenth century is quoted as saying about his cat:

> When my cat and I entertain each other with mutual apish tricks, as playing with a garter, who knows but I make my cat more sport than she makes me? Shall I conclude her to be single, that has her time to begin or refuse to play as freely as I myself have? Nay, who knows but that it is a defect of my not understanding her language (for doubtless cats talk and reason with one another) that we agree no better? And who knows but that she pities me for being no wiser than to play with her, and laughs and censures my folly for making sport for her, when we two play together?

Ever since the Middle Ages when the cat was in public disgrace because people, in their religious fervor, thought the cat to be a devil or to be associated with the devil and witches, there has been a flood of writing about cats. Hardly a month goes by that a new book is not published which has something to do with cats.

One of the earliest references to the cat in English literature is in a poem called "Pangur Ban," written in the ninth century by an Irish scholar. The monk tells how he and his cat are much alike, each pursuing his own tasks alone: The monk pursues words, while the cat pursues rats.

In the tenth century, the Prince of south Wales, Hywel Dda, or Howel the Good, issued laws which told what a cat is worth. Howel's laws show that he had respect for kittens and cats and the work that they could do. "The worth of a kitten from the night it is kittened until it shall open its eyes is a legal penny. And from that time until it shall kill mice, two legal pence. And after it shall kill mice four legal pence. And so it will always remain.

"Her tiethi [qualities] are to see, to hear, to kill mice, to have her claws entire, to rear and not devour her kittens, and if she be bought and be deficient in any one of these tiethi, let one third of her worth be returned." Of course, a penny in those days was worth a great deal more than it is now.

Another extract from Howel the Good's codes indicates

> "the animals whose tail, eyes and life are of equal worth: a calf, a filly from common work and a cat, excepting the cat that shall watch the King's barn."

The cat who watched over the royal barn was worth more than other cats:

> Whoever shall kill a cat that guards a house and a barn of the King, or shall take it stealthily, it is to be held with its head to the ground and its tail up, the ground being swept, and then clean wheat is to be poured about it, until the tip of its tail be hidden; and that is its worth.

Geoffrey Chaucer mentioned the cat occasionally in his *Canterbury Tales.* In "The Maunciple's Tale," Chaucer wrote about a cat's decided preference for mice over milk, meat, or any other dainty tidbit:

> Lat take a cat, and fostre hym wel with milk
> And tendre flessche, and make his couche of silk,
> And lat hym seen a mous go by the wal;

Anon he weyvith milk, and flessche, and al,
And every deyntee that is in that hous,
Swich appetyt hath he to ete a mous.

William Shakespeare called the domestic pussycat "the harmless, necessary cat," which is not a particularly flattering description, but then Shakespeare was living in the Elizabethan age when having cats as pets was not as popular as it became later on.

Samuel Johnson was sure that cats had feelings. James Boswell included this passage about Hodge, the great doctor's cat, in his biography:

> I recollect him one day scrambling up Dr. Johnson's breast, apparently with much satisfaction, while my friend, smiling and half-whistling, rubbed down his back, and pulled him by the tail; and when I observed he was a fine cat, saying, "Why, yes, Sir, but I have had cats whom I liked better than this"; and then, as if perceiving Hodge to be out of countenance, adding, "but he is a very fine cat, a very fine cat indeed."

Boswell also writes, "I shall never forget the indulgence with which he treated Hodge, his cat, for whom he himself used to go out and buy oysters lest the servants, having that trouble, should take a dislike to the poor creature. . . ."

From the nineteenth century onward, more and more people began to write about cats. Colette, the famous French woman of letters who died in 1954, adored cats and wrote about them in numerous stories. Colette said that she loved cats almost more than people, and her observations of the domestic pet were especially keen. She wrote a splendid short story about a cat named Saha in which the feelings of the cat are poignantly revealed: Saha is terrorized in the story by a person who forces her onto a window ledge from which there is no escape except an almost certainly fatal jump to the ground; the cat grows so nervous that she leaves wet paw prints on the ledge—cats perspire from their feet when they are frightened. Saha miraculously survives the jump, but the suspense is almost unbearable. Colette said that the character of the gentle Saha was based upon one of her own cats.

Mark Twain once said that if man could be crossed with the cat, it would probably improve man, although the crossing might do great harm to the cat species. All his life, Twain kept cats, and he probably had a higher opinion of their good qualities than he had of most men and women. Twain also wrote, "A home without a cat, and a well-fed, well-petted, and properly revered cat, may be a perfect home, *perhaps,* but how can it prove its title?"

T. S. Eliot loved cats and even wrote a whole book of verse about them called *Old Possum's Book of Practical Cats.* Most critics and poetry lovers feel that the poems Old Possum wrote are doggerel, poor poetry indeed, but certainly the lines are all-time favorites with cat fanciers. Eliot felt that cats have particularly sensitive natures. His poem on how to address a cat shows that he thought it very important that a stranger approach a cat with dignity and that a man shouldn't be too familiar with any cat right at the start of a friendship. Cats are naturally dignified and probably don't like to be shouted at—"Hey you!"—or even tickled and petted and called baby names before a proper introduction.

The Ad-Dressing of Cats

by T. S. Eliot

You've read of several kinds of Cat,
And my opinion now is that
You should need no interpreter
To understand their character.
You now have learned enough to see
That Cats are much like you and me
And other people whom we find
Possessed of various types of mind.
For some are sane and some are mad
And some are good and some are bad
And some are better, some are worse—
But all may be described in verse.
You've seen them both at work and games,
And learnt about their proper names,
Their habits and their habitat:
But
How would you ad-dress a Cat?

So first, your memory I'll jog,
And say: A CAT IS NOT A DOG.

Now dogs pretend they like to fight;
They often bark, more seldom bite;
But yet a Dog is, on the whole,
What you would call a simple soul.
Of course I'm not including Pekes,
And such fantastic canine freaks.

The usual Dog about the Town
Is much inclined to play the clown,
And far from showing too much pride
Is frequently undignified.
He's very easily taken in—
Just chuck him underneath the chin
Or slap his back or shake his paw,
And he will gambol and guffaw.
He's such an easy-going lout,
He'll answer any hail or shout.

Again I must remind you that
A Dog's a Dog—A CAT'S A CAT.

With Cats, some say, one rule is true:
Don't speak till you are spoken to.
Myself, I do not hold with that—
I say, you should ad-dress a Cat.
But always keep in mind that he
Resents familiarity.
I bow, and taking off my hat,
Ad-dress him in this form: O CAT!
But if he is the Cat next door,
Whom I have often met before
(He comes to see me in my flat)
I greet him with an OOPSA CAT!
I think I've heard them call him James—
But we've not got so far as names.
Before a Cat will condescend
To treat you as a trusted friend,
Some little token of esteem

Is needed, like a dish of cream;
And you might now and then supply
Some caviare, or Strassburg Pie,
Some potted grouse, or salmon paste—
He's sure to have his personal taste.
(I know a Cat, who makes a habit
Of eating nothing else but rabbit,
And when he's finished, licks his paws
So's not to waste the onion sauce.)
A Cat's entitled to expect
These evidences of respect.
And so in time you reach your aim,
And finally call him by his NAME.

So this is this, and that is that:
And there's how you AD-DRESS A CAT.

The list of people who have written about cats could go on and on—Victor Hugo, Alexandre Dumas, Thomas Gray, William Wordsworth, Walter de la Mare, Algernon Charles Swinburne, William Butler Yeats, Thomas Hardy, John Keats, Dame Edith Sitwell, and hundreds of other poets; Sir Winston Churchill, Compton MacKenzie, Carl Van Vechten, Sheila Burnford, and many, many other authors. In fact, a large dictionary compiled by Christabel Lady Aberconway tells all about famous and not-so-famous men and women who loved and wrote about cats; the book is called, appropriately, *A Dictionary of Cat Lovers,* and a second revised edition has recently been published. In a review of Lady Aberconway's revised dictionary, Anthony Burgess, the distinguished contemporary British novelist, wrote, "We can't imagine God as a dog, but He may well be a cat with (Old Possum's words) an ineffable name." Taken out of the context of the author's review in the *Spectator* magazine, the sentence may shock a few people, but certainly not cat lovers, who would immediately understand that a joke had been made and that no disrespect for God was intended. Many people feel that the cat is an excellent symbol for a dignified, omnipotent presence; and writers have often expressed that feeling.

There are two other special cat stories which deserve a mention and which can be thoroughly enjoyed only in reading them complete. One is Paul Gallico's book *Jennie.* It is the story of a little boy who is turned into a cat, and, with the help of Jennie, a kindly motherly adult cat, the boy-cat learns how to behave in a catlike manner. One of the funniest sections in the book concerns Jennie's teaching Peter to keep himself clean; Peter has an exceedingly difficult time learning how to stretch and lick himself all over, but Jennie explains in careful detail exactly how to wash from his forehead to the tip of his tail.

Edgar Allan Poe wrote a fascinating and horrifying tale called "The Black Cat." It is doubtful that even medieval people who were terrified of witches' cats could have dreamed up so frightening a vision of a cat. "The Black Cat" perfectly mirrors the feelings of all those people who have a cat phobia; cat lovers should only read the story on a bright, cheerful and sunny day, preferably with a friend close at hand.

A writer who is not so famous, except in his native Germany, wrote a whole delightful diary of a cat called *The*

Opinions of Tom Cat Murr. E. T. A. Hoffmann, who lived in the late eighteenth and early nineteenth century, was especially fond of cats; his cat diary was actually written as two stories in one—half of the book explains the philosophies and cultural opinions of a chapel master, and the other half explains how the cat thinks. The chapter which follows is Tom Cat Murr's explanation of how he came to write and the difficulties he experienced. Murr is certainly one of the vainest of cats, and he thinks that he is a genius.

from The Opinions of Tom Cat Murr

by E. T. A. Hoffman

Nothing attracted me in my master's study more than his writing table loaded with books, papers and all manner of strange implements. I might even say that this table was a magic circle which drew me as if by a magic spell, yet I felt a certain awe that prevented me from succumbing completely to my desire to investigate.

At last one day, at a moment when my master was out, I overcame my fear and jumped up onto the table. My rapture was intense as I sat there rummaging about among the books and papers. It was not wantonness, indeed, but impatience, a burning scientific curiosity, that caused me to seize a manuscript in my paws and pull it about until it lay torn to shreds in front of me. My master came in and seeing what had happened, set upon me with the exclamation: "Accursed brute!" He thrashed me so severely that, crying with pain, I crept under the stove and for the rest of that day would not be tempted out, however kind the invitation.

Such an incident might well have been enough to deter anyone from pursuing the course ordained for him by nature; genius in men is, in fact, often arrested by such an unpleasant experience. But no sooner had I fully recovered from my pain than, following my irresistible urge, I again jumped onto the writing table. To be sure, it needed but one shout from my master, an unfinished sentence, for example: "Scat . . . you . . . !" to chase me off, so that I got no time for study. I waited patiently, however, for a favorable moment to begin my studies and this was not long in coming.

One day while my master was preparing to go out, I concealed myself so well that he failed to find me when he remembered the torn manuscript and wished to chase me out of the room. Barely had my master left, than I sprang at one bound onto the table and settled down among the papers. An indescribable sense of well-being overcame me.

With my paws, I deftly opened a sizeable book that lay before me, and tried to see if I could understand the characters it contained. At first I was utterly unsuccessful, but instead of giving up I stared at the pages, expecting that by some very special inspiration, I should learn to read. Thus engrossed, I was surprised by my master. With a loud: "Confound that beast!" he sprang toward me. It was too late to save myself, and I flattened my ears and cowered down as far as I could, expecting at any moment to feel the stick on my back.

But with his hand already raised, my master suddenly

paused, laughed out loud and cried, "Cat, cat, are you reading? Now that I will not forbid you. Let us see, then, what kind of thirst for knowledge you have." He pulled the book from under my clutching paws, looked at it and began laughing again. "Well, I must say," he observed, "you seem to have got together a small reference library, for otherwise I cannot imagine how that book comes to be on my writing table. Well then, go on reading. Study diligently, cat. Oh, and if necessary you may mark important passages in the book with small scratches." And he pushed the open book back in front of me.

It was, as I later discovered, a book called *On Human Relations* and I have derived much worldly wisdom from it. It expresses exactly my innermost feelings, and is altogether extraordinarily suitable for cats who wish to make some mark in human society. This aspect of the book has, so far as I know, been overlooked hitherto.

From that time on, my master made me welcome whenever I jumped up and settled among the papers before him when he himself was at work.

My master's son was often called upon to read aloud for long periods at a time. On these occasions I did not fail to place myself so that I could see the page he was reading. I was able to do this without annoyance to him, being endowed by nature with keen-sighted eyes. Thus, by comparing the characters with the words he spoke I learned in a short time to read. Anyone who happens to think this incredible has no inkling of the altogether exceptional ingenuity bestowed on me by nature. Those who understand and esteem me highly will harbor no doubts regarding my kind of education—equal, perhaps, to their own.

Here I must not forget to mention the remarkable observation I made respecting my complete understanding of human speech. Although in full consciousness, I have no idea how I arrived at this understanding of speech. This is also said to be the case with humans, and does not in the least surprise me, for during the years of childhood, the human race is much more stupid and helpless than ours. Even as a very small kitten, I never scratched my eyes, tried to take hold of the fire or of a lamp, or ate shoe polish instead of strawberry jam, as small children do.

Being now able to read perfectly, and becoming daily more and more filled with the thoughts of various scholars, I felt the irresistible urge to save from oblivion my thoughts which were born of my innermost genius. This, however, demanded the admittedly very difficult art of writing. However attentively I might watch my master's hand when he was writing, the actual mechanics of his art continued to elude me. I studied the only writing manual my master possessed, and had almost concluded that the mysterious difficulty of writing could only be surmounted by means of the large cuff which surrounded the wrist of the writing hand pictured in the book. I realized that it was solely my master's degree of proficiency that allowed him to write without a cuff, in the same way as a practiced tightrope walker can eventually dispense with a balancing pole. I thought longingly of cuffs, and was about to purloin the old housekeeper's nightcap to adapt it for my right paw, when suddenly, in a moment of inspiration, such as men (or cats) of genius experience, I lit on the brilliant idea that was to solve everything.

I surmised that the impossibility of holding a pen or pencil as my master did might lie in the different construction of our hands, and this supposition proved correct. I had to devise another manner of writing, suited to the construction of my small right paw. And find a new method I did, as may well be imagined. This is how great inventions and discoveries are born.

Another grave difficulty for me was how to dip the pen into the inkpot. For I was unable to keep my paw clean during this operation since it always got into the ink as well. The first strokes, made with my paw rather than with the pen, always appeared smudged and sprawling. This might lead foolish people to see in my first manuscripts little more than paper spattered with ink. But, the intelligent man will readily detect in those early works a cat of great depth, and will be astonished, even delighted, by the profundity and the richness of intellect which came gushing from its inexhaustible spring.

So that the world, and especially critics and students, in days to come may not quarrel over the chronological order of my immortal works, I will say now that my first book was the philosophical, sentimental, didactic novel *Thought and Presentiment, or Cat and Dog*. This work could by itself have caused a great stir. Next, being able to turn my hand to anything, I wrote a political work entitled *Of Mousetraps, and Their Influence on the Attitude and the Enterprise of Cats,* and following upon this, I felt inspired to write the tragedy *Cawdallor, King of Rats.* This tragedy, had it been presented times without number in all imaginable theaters, would have received the most tumultuous applause and wide popularity. These products of my ambitious spirit were but the forerunners of the whole range of my collected works, and at the appropriate place I shall explain my reasons for writing them.

When I had learned to hold the pen and to keep my paw free of ink, my style acquired greater charm, grace and clarity. I devoted myself especially to poetry and wrote a number of agreeable pieces. Even at that time I nearly wrote a heroic poem in twenty-four cantos, but before I had finished, it turned into something quite different. For this, the prominent poets of today are probably very grateful.

Cat Murr (his mark)

The observations about cats made by poets and writers are often very expressive of the cat's personality. The following brief selections are the works of people who are either confirmed cat lovers or cat haters. Whether one or the other, they were compelled by the personality of the cat to put down their feelings and thoughts about the fascinating creature.

On a Favourite Cat, Drowned in a Tub of Gold Fishes

by Thomas Gray

'Twas on a lofty vase's side,
Where China's gayest art had dyed

The azure flowers that blow,
Demurest of the tabby kind
The pensive Selima, reclined,
Gazed on the lake below.

Her conscious tail her joy declared:
The fair round face, the snowy beard,
The velvet of her paws,
Her coat that with the tortoise vies,
Her ears of jet, and emerald eyes—
She saw, and purr'd applause.

Still had she gazed, but 'midst the tide
Two angel forms were seen to glide,
The Genii of the stream:
Their scaly armour's Tyrian hue
Through richest purple, to the view
Betray'd a golden gleam.

The hapless Nymph with wonder saw:
A whisker first, and then a claw
With many an ardent wish
She stretch'd, in vain, to reach the prize—
What female heart can gold despise?
What Cat's averse to fish?

Presumptuous maid! with looks intent
Again she stretch'd, again she bent,
Nor knew the gulf between—
Malignant Fate sat by and smiled—

The slippery verge her feet beguiled;
She tumbled headlong in!

Eight times emerging from the flood
She mew'd to every watery God
Some speedy aid to send:—
No Dolphin came, no Nereid stirr'd,
Nor cruel Tom nor Susan heard—
A favourite has no friend!

From hence, ye Beauties! undeceived
Know one false step is ne'er retrieved,
And be with caution bold:
Not all that tempts your wandering eyes
And heedless hearts, is lawful prize,
Nor all that glisters, gold!

The Kitten Playing with the Fallen Leaves

by William Wordsworth

See the kitten on the wall
Sporting with the leaves that fall!
Withered leaves, one, two, and three,
From the lofty elder-tree.
Through the calm and frosty air
Of this morning bright and fair
Eddying round and round they sink
Softly, slowly. One might think,
From the motions that are made,
Every little leaf conveyed

Some small fairy, hither tending,
To this lower world descending.
—But the kitten how she starts!
Crouches, stretches, paws, and darts:
First at one, and then its fellow,
Just as light, and just as yellow:
There are many now—now one—
Now they stop and there are none.
What intentness of desire
In her upturned eye of fire!
With a tiger leap halfway,
Now she meets the coming prey.
Lets it go at last, and then
Has it in her power again.

Feelings
by Melville Cane

The cat killed a rat.
Magnificent in conquest
It lay basking.
How splendid the cat!
How horrid, how venomous the rat!
I breathed heavy with exultation
Over my enemy
Stiff and ugly in the dust.

It was no rat;
It was a baby rabbit,
Warmness running out.

Tender, curving back!
Soft, pathetic fur!
Innocent, wondering eyes!

The proud cat crumples and slinks,
Wind rips the roses,
A cloud bags the sun.

The Cat and the Moon

by William Butler Yeats

The cat went here and there
And the moon spun round like a top,
And the nearest kin of the moon,
The creeping cat, looked up.
Black Minnaloushe stared at the moon,
For, wander and wail as he would,
The pure cold light in the sky
Troubled his animal blood.
Minnaloushe runs in the grass
Lifting his delicate feet.
Do you dance, Minnaloushe, do you dance?
When two close kindred meet,
What better than call a dance?
Maybe the moon may learn,
Tired of that courtly fashion,
A new dance turn.
Minnaloushe creeps through the grass
From moonlit place to place,
The sacred moon overhead

Has taken a new phase.
Does Minnaloushe know that his pupils
Will pass from change to change,
And that from round to crescent,
From crescent to round they range?
Minnaloushe creeps through the grass
Alone, important and wise,
And lifts to the changing moon
His changing eyes.

Henry Fielding, the English novelist, wrote a short account of the near-fatal accident of a ship's kitten in his travel diary, *A Voyage to Lisbon.* The incident is particularly interesting, for Fielding remarks on the old sailor's superstition that a drowning cat will raise favorable sailing winds.

> *Thursday, July 11th, 1754.* A most tragical incident fell out this day at sea. While the ship was under sail, but making as will appear no great way, a kitten, one of four of the feline inhabitants of the cabin, fell from the window into the water: an alarm was immediately given to the captain, who was then upon deck, and received it with the utmost concern and many bitter oaths. He immediately gave orders to the steersman in favour of the poor thing, as he called it; the sails were instantly slackened, and all hands, as the phrase is, employed to recover the poor animal. I was, I own, extremely surprised at all this; less indeed at the captain's extreme tenderness than at his conceiving any possibility of success; for if puss had had nine thousand instead of nine lives, I concluded they had been

all lost. The boatswain, however, had more sanguine hopes, for having stripped himself of his jacket, breeches and shirt, he leaped boldly into the water, and to my great astonishment, in a few minutes returned to the ship, bearing the motionless animal in his mouth. Nor was this, I observed, a matter of such great difficulty as it appeared to my ignorance, and possibly may seem to that of my fresh-water reader. The kitten was now exposed to air and sun on the deck, where its life, of which it retained no symptoms, was despaired of by all.

But as I have, perhaps, a little too wantonly endeavoured to raise the tender passions of my readers in this narrative, I should think myself unpardonable if I concluded it without giving them the satisfaction of hearing that the kitten at last recovered, to the great joy of the good captain, but to the great disappointment of some of the sailors, who asserted that the drowning cat was the very surest way of raising a favourable wind; a supposition of which, though we have heard several plausible accounts, we will not presume to assign the true original reason.

The literature about cats includes, of course, the hundreds of nursery and nonsense rhymes which have been printed over the years to amuse children. The popularity of the funny singsong verses extends far beyond the nursery, for older children and adults remember them, too. The rhymes about pussy cats have been repeated to children for a hundred years or more in the following versions, but scholars have traced some of the verses as far back as ancient Greek and Latin literature.

I love little pussy,
Her coat is so warm,
And if I don't hurt her
She'll do me no harm.
So I'll not pull her tail,
Nor drive her away,
But pussy and I
Very gently will play.

Pussy cat, pussy cat,
Where have you been?
I've been to London
To look at the Queen.
Pussy cat, pussy cat,
What did you there?
I frightened a little mouse
Under her chair.

Sing, sing,
What shall I sing?
The cat's run away
With the pudding string!
Do, do,
What shall I do?
The cat's run away
With the pudding too!

Ding, dong, bell,
Pussy's in the well.
Who put her in?
Little Johnny Green.
Who pulled her out?

Little Tommy Stout.
What a naughty boy was that
To try to drown poor pussy cat,
Who never did him any harm,
And killed the mice in his father's barn.

Hey, diddle, diddle!
The cat and the fiddle,
The cow jumped over the moon;
The little dog laughed
To see such sport,
And the dish ran away with the spoon.

A Latin version of the favorite "Hey, diddle, diddle" rhyme was printed by John Halliwell in his *The Nursery Rhymes of England* in 1842. Roman children of long ago may have said this in gay singsong voices to themselves or even repeated it in their early school days.

Hei didulum! atque iterum didulum! Felisque fidesque
  Vacca super lunae cornua prosiluit;
Nescio qua catulus risit dulcedine ludi;
  Abstulit et turpi lanx cochleare fuga.

The Owl and the Pussy-cat
by Edward Lear

The Owl and the Pussy-cat went to sea
  In a beautiful pea-green boat;
They took some honey, and plenty of money
Wrapped up in a five-pound note.

The Owl looked up to the stars above,
  And sang to a small guitar,
"O lovely Pussy! O Pussy, my love,
  What a beautiful Pussy you are!
      You are,
      You are,
  What a beautiful Pussy you are!"

Pussy said to the Owl, "You elegant fowl!
  How charmingly sweet you sing!
O let us be married! too long we have tarried:
  But what shall we do for a ring?"
They sailed away, for a year and a day,
  To the land where the Bong-tree grows,
And there in a wood a Piggy-wig stood
  With a ring at the end of his nose.
      His nose,
      His nose,
  With a ring at the end of his nose.

"Dear Pig, are you willing to sell for one shilling
  Your ring?" Said the Piggy, "I will."
So they took it away, and were married next day
By the Turkey who lives on the hill.
They dined on mince and slices of quince,
  Which they ate with a runcible spoon;
And hand in hand, on the edge of the sand,
  They danced by the light of the moon.
      The moon,
      The moon,
They danced by the light of the moon.

Kitty: What She Thinks of Herself

by William Brighty Rands

I am the Cat of Cats. I am
The everlasting cat!
Cunning and old and sleek as jam,
The everlasting cat!
I hunt the vermin in the night—
The everlasting cat!
For I see best without the light—
The everlasting cat!

Arthur Weigall wrote the true tale of Basta, a cat whose lineage stretched back to ancient Egyptian days and who made friends with man but in the end preferred to remain a creature who walked by "its wild lone." Weigall was Inspector-General of Antiquities to the Egyptian Government from 1905 to 1914. He was a prominent English Egyptologist, familiar with all the lore of Egyptian holy cats. The story of Basta is taken from Weigall's book *Laura Was My Camel,* reminiscences of the weird collection of animals which formed part of the author's household in Egypt.

Basta seems the epitome of all cats, ancient and modern. She is a cat who may truly look at a king, a cat who is not only descended from the gods, but a cat's cat, too.

Basta, a Holy Cat of Bubastis

by Arthur Weigall

One summer during a heat-wave, when the temperature in the shade of my verandah in Luxor was a hundred and twenty-five degrees Fahrenheit, I went down to cooler Lower Egypt to pay a visit to an English friend of mine stationed at Zagazig, the native city which stands beside the ruins of ancient Bubastis.

He was about to leave Egypt, and asked me whether I would like to have his cat, a dignified, mystical-minded, long-legged, small-headed, green-eyed female, whose orange-yellow hair, marked with grayish-black stripes in tabby pattern, was so short that she gave the impression of being naked—an impression, however, which did not in any way detract from her air of virginal chastity.

Her name was Basta, and though her more recent ancestors had lived wild amongst the ruins, she was so obviously a descendant of the holy cats of ancient times, who were incarnations of the goddess Basta, that I thought it only right to accept the offer and take her up to Luxor to live with me. To be the expert in charge of Egyptian antiquities, and not to have an ancient Egyptian cat to give an air of mystery to my headquarters, had, indeed, always seemed to me to be somewhat wanting in showmanship on my part.

Thus it came about that on my departure I drove off to the railroad station with the usually dignified Basta bumping about and uttering unearthly howls inside a cardboard hat-box, in the side of which I had cut a small round hole for ventilation. The people in the streets and on the station platform seemed to be under the impression that the noises were digestive and that I was in dire need of a doctor; and it was a great relief to my embarrassment when the hot and panting train steamed in.

Fortunately I found myself alone in the compartment, and the hat-box on the seat at my side had begun to cause me less anxiety, when suddenly Basta was seized with a sort of religious frenzy. The box rocked about, and presently out through the air-hole came a long, snake-like paw which waved weirdly to and fro in space for a moment, and then was withdrawn, its place being taken by a pink nose which pushed itself outwards with such frantic force that the sides of the hole gave way, and out burst the entire sandy, sacred head.

She then began to choke, for the cardboard was pressing tightly around her neck; and to save her from strangulation I was obliged to tear the aperture open, whereupon she wriggled out, leapt in divine frenzy up the side of the carriage, and prostrated herself on the net-work of the baggage-rack, where her hysteria caused her to lose all control of herself, and if I say modestly that she was overcome with nausea I shall be telling but a part of the dreadful tale.

The rest of the journey was like a bad dream; but at the Cairo terminus where I had to change into the night express for Luxor I got the help of a native policeman who secured a large laundry basket from the sleeping-car department, and after a prolonged struggle, during which the train was shunted into a distant siding, we managed somehow to imprison the struggling Basta once more.

The perspiring policeman and I then carried the basket at a run along the tracks back to the station in the sweltering heat of the late afternoon, and I just managed to catch my train; but during this second part of my journey Basta traveled in the baggage-van, whence, in the hot and silent night, whenever we were at a standstill, her appalling incantations came drifting to my ears.

I opened the basket in an unfurnished spare room in my house, and like a flash Basta was up the bare wall and onto the curtain-pole above the window. There she remained all day in a sort of mystic trance, but at sunset the saucer of milk and plate of fish which I had provided for her at last enticed her down, and in the end she reconciled herself to her new surroundings, and indicated by her behaviour that she was willing to accept my house as her earthly temple.

With Pedro, my pariah dog, there was not the slightest trouble: he had no strong feelings about cats, and she on her part graciously deigned to acknowledge his status—as, I believe, is generally the case in native households. She sometimes condescended to visit my horse and donkey in their stalls; and for Laura, my camel, she quickly developed a real regard, often sleeping for hours in her stable—perhaps because at that time they were both unmarried girls and had their innocence and its hopes in common.

I was not worried as to how she would treat the chickens and pigeons, because her former owner at Zagazig had insisted upon her respecting his hen-coop and pigeon-cote; but I was a little anxious about the ducks, for she had not previously known any, and in ancient times her ancestors used to be trained to hunt wild geese and ducks and were fed with pâté de foie gras on holy days and anniversaries.

In a corner of the garden I had made a miniature duck-pond which was sunk rather deeply in the ground and down to which I had cut a narrow, steeply sloping passage or gangway. During the day, after the ducks had been up and down this slope several times, the surface used to become wet and slippery, and the ducks, having waddled down the first few inches, were forced to toboggan down the rest of it on their tails, with their two feet sticking out in front of them and their heads well up.

Basta was always fascinated by this slide and by the splash at the bottom, and used to sit and watch it all for hours, which made me think at first that she would one day spring at one of them; but she never did. Field-mice, and water-rats down by the Nile, were her only prey; and in connection with the former I may mention a curious occurrence.

One hot night I was sitting smoking my pipe on the verandah, when my attention was attracted by two mice which had crept into the patch of brilliant moonlight before my feet, and were boldly nibbling some crumbs left over from a cracker thrown to Pedro earlier in the evening. I watched them silently for a while and did not notice that Basta had seen them and was preparing to spring, nor did I observe a large white owl sitting aloft amongst the overhanging roses and also preparing to pounce.

Suddenly, and precisely at the same moment, the owl shot down on the mice from above and Basta leapt at them from beside me. There was a collision and a wild scuffle; fur and feathers flew; I fell out of my chair; and then the owl made off screeching in one direction and the cat dashed away in the other; while the mice, practically clinging to one another, remained for a moment or so too terrified to move.

During the early days of her residence in Luxor, Basta often used to go down to the edge of the Nile to fish with her paw; but she never caught anything, and in the end she got a fright and gave it up.

I was sitting by the river one morning watching her trying to catch one of a little shoal of small fish which were sunning themselves in the shallow water, when there came swimming into view a twelve-or-fourteen-inch fish which I recognized (by its whiskers and the absence of a dorsal fin) as the electric cat-fish pretty common in the Nile—a strange creature able to give you an electric shock like hitting your funnybone.

These fish obtain their food in a curious way: they hang around any shoal of small fry engaged in feeding, and then glide quietly into their midst and throw out this electric shock, whereupon the little fellows are all sick to the stomach, and the big fellow gets their disgorged dinners.

I was just waiting to see this happen with my own eyes —for it had always seemed a bit far-fetched—when Basta made a dart at the intruder with her paw, and got a shock. She uttered a yowl as though somebody had trodden on her, and leapt high in the air; and never again did she put her foot near the water. She was content after that with our daily offering of a fish brought from the market and fried for her like a burnt sacrifice.

My bedroom was on the ground floor of my house, and as I used to leave the long-windows open, Basta often wandered into the room in the night and jumped onto my bed, smelling faintly of Laura's stable. Pedro used also to come in occasionally, and when they met in the darkness there was generally a little quiet hissing and growling, though hardly enough to wake me up; but when there was a moon and the room was not quite dark they used sometimes to catch sight of themselves in the long mirror, and I would then be violently awakened either by Pedro's ferocious barking or by Basta's savage yowls.

Neither of them would ever do this in the daytime, because they knew then that what they saw was only their own reflection; but at night the illusion was more convincing, and they never ceased to be deceived by it.

Basta had a most unearthly voice, and when she was feeling emotional she would let out a wail which at first was like the crying of a phantom baby, and then became the tuneless song of a lunatic, and finally developed into the blood-curdling howl of a soul in torment. And when she spat the percussion was like that of a spring-gun.

There were some wild cats, or, rather, domestic cats who, like Basta's own forebears, had taken to a wild life, living in a grove of trees beside the river just beyond my garden wall; and it was generally the proximity of one of these which started her off, but sometimes the outburst was caused by her own unfathomable thoughts as she went her mysterious ways in the darkness of the night.

I think she must have been clairvoyant, for she often seemed to be seeing things not visible to me. Sometimes, perhaps when she was cleaning fish or mouse from her face, she would pause with one foot off the ground and stare in front of her, and then back away with bristling hair or go forward with friendly little mewing noises; and sometimes she would leap off a chair or sofa, her tail lashing and her green eyes dilated. But it may have been worms.

Once I saw her standing absolutely rigid and tense on the lawn, staring at the rising moon; and then all of a sudden she did a sort of dance such as cats sometimes do when they are playing with other cats. But there was no other cat, and, anyway, Basta never played: she never forgot that she was a holy cat.

Her chaste hauteur was so great that she would not move out of the way when people were walking about, and many a time her demoniacal shriek, and perhaps a crash of breaking glass, informed the household that somebody had tripped over her. It was astonishing, however, how quickly she recovered her dignity and how well she maintained the pretense that whatever happened to her was at her own celestial wish and was not our doing.

If I called her she would pretend not to hear, but would come a few moments later when it could appear that she had thought of doing so first; and if I lifted her off a chair she would jump back onto it and then descend with dignity as though of her own free will. But in this, of course, she was more like a woman than like a divinity.

The Egyptian cat is a domesticated species of the African wild-cat, and no doubt its strange behaviour and its weird voice were the cause of its being regarded as sacred in ancient times; but although the old gods and their worship have been forgotten these many centuries, the traditional sanctity of the race has survived. Modern Egyptians think it unlucky to hurt a cat, and in the native quarters of Cairo and other cities hundreds of cats are daily fed at the expense of benevolent citizens. They say that they do this because cats are so useful to mankind in killing off mice and other pests; but actually it is an unrecognized survival of the old beliefs.

In the days of the Pharaohs, when a cat died the men of the household shaved off their eyebrows and sat around wailing and rocking themselves to and fro in simulated anguish. The body was embalmed and buried with solemn rites in the local cats' cemetery, or was sent down to Bubastis to rest in the shadow of the temple of their patron goddess. I myself have dug up hundreds of mummified cats; and once, in fact, when I had a couple of dozen of the best specimens standing on my verandah waiting to be despatched to the Cairo Museum, Basta was most excited about it, and walked around sniffing at them all day. They certainly smelt awful.

Egyptian cats—living ones, I mean—were imported into ancient Greece and Italy by Phoenician traders, and became the part-ancestors of most of the European breeds; but Basta, who was of the pure Bubastis stock, was nevertheless quite unlike any cats at home. She was so lanky, her head was so small for her body, her yellow fur was so stiff and short and made her look so undressed, and she was so eminently uncanny.

On my lawn there was a square slab of stone which had once been the top of an altar dedicated to the sun-god, but was now used as a sort of low garden table; and sometimes when she had caught a mouse she used to deposit the chewed corpse upon this slab—nobody could think why, unless, as I always told people, she was really making an offering to the sun. It was most mysterious of her; but it led once to a very unfortunate episode.

A famous French antiquarian, who was paying a polite call, was sitting with me beside this sacred stone drinking afternoon tea and eating fresh dates, when Basta appeared on the scene with a small dead mouse in her mouth, which in her usual way she deposited upon the slab—only on this occasion she laid it on my guest's plate which was standing on the slab.

We were talking at the moment and did not see her do this, and anyhow the Frenchman was as blind as a bat; and, of course, as luck would have it, he immediately picked up the wet, mole-coloured mouse instead of a ripe brown date, and the thing had almost gone into his mouth before he saw what it was and, with a yell, flung it into the air.

It fell into his upturned sun-helmet which was lying on the grass beside him; but he did not see where it had gone, and jumping angrily to his feet in the momentary belief that I had played a school-boy joke on him, he snatched up his helmet and was in the act of putting it on his head when the mouse tumbled out onto the front of his shirt and slipped down inside his buttoned jacket.

At this he went more or less mad, danced about, shook himself, and finally trod on Basta who completed his frenzy by uttering a fiendish howl and digging her claws into his leg. The dead mouse, I am glad to say, fell onto the grass during the dance without passing through his roomy trousers as I had feared it might; and Basta, recovering her dignity, picked it up and walked off with it.

It is a remarkable fact that during the five or six years

she spent with me she showed no desire to be anything but a spinster all her life, and when I arranged a marriage for her she displayed such dignified but violent antipathy towards the bridegroom that the match was a failure. In the end, however, she fell in love with one of the wild cats who lived amongst the trees beyond my wall, and nothing could prevent her going off to visit him from time to time, generally at dead of night.

He did not care a hoot about her sanctity, and she was feminine enough to enjoy the novelty of being roughly treated. I never actually saw him, for he did not venture into the garden, but I used to hear him knocking her about outside my gates; and when she came home scratched and bitten and muttering something about holy cats, it was plain that she was desperately happy. She licked her wounds, indeed, with deep and voluptuous satisfaction.

A dreadful change came over her. She had lost her precious dignity, and was restless and inclined to be savage; her digestion played embarrassing tricks on her; and once she mortally offended Laura by clawing her nose. There was a new glint in her green eyes as she watched the ducks sliding into the pond; the pigeons interested her for the first time; and for the first time, too, she ate the mice she had caught.

Then she began to disappear for a whole day or night at a time, and once when I went in search of her amongst the trees outside and found her sharpening her claws on a branch above my head, she put her ears back and hissed at me until I could see every one of her teeth and halfway down her pink throat. I tried by every method to keep her at home when she came back, but it was all in vain, and at last she left me forever.

Weeks afterwards I caught sight of her once again amongst the trees, and it was evident that she was soon to become a mother. She gave me a friendly little mew this time, but she would not let me touch her; and presently she slipped away into the undergrowth. I never knew what became of her.

The cat has existed for thousands of years. It is more than likely that the creature will exist for thousands and thousands of years to come. It is even possible that man will learn to communicate with the cat and perhaps at last understand what it is about the animal that makes it eternally fascinating.

Sir Walter Scott wrote a few words about the cat that express as succinctly and well as almost anyone can why there was a cult of the cat and why there is a cat fancy:

"Cats are a mysterious kind of folk. There is more passing in their minds than we are aware of."

Human beings seek answers to whatever is mysterious. But the cat prefers to keep its secrets and to remain always independent.

A FRAGMENT OF FRIENDSHIP

A memory of Evelyn Waugh when young

by

Dudley Carew

EVEREST BOOKS LIMITED

4 Valentine Place, London, S.E.1

Published in Great Britain by Everest Books Limited, 1974
ISBN: 0 903925 10 9

Set in Monotype Baskerville
Printed in Great Britain by
The Anchor Press Ltd,
Tiptree, Essex

Foreword

Evelyn at Lancing

1921

Evelyn at Underhill and Elsewhere

1921–1931

By the Same Author:

Autobiography

The House Is Gone

Novels

The Next Corner
Tuesday, Wednesday, Thursday
The Courteous Revelation
The Son Of Grief
The Taken Town
The Puppet's Part

Cricket Books

England Over
To The Wicket

To

E.A.St: J.W.

as I knew him

Grateful acknowledgements are due to David Pryce-Jones and Weidenfeld and Nicolson for permission to publish here certain pages which appeared in the book *Evelyn Waugh and His World.*

Foreword

A short time ago Mr Cyril Connolly recorded his sense of shock when he came across a document, in Evelyn Waugh's handwriting, in one of his own books which consisted of page after page of disapproval, hate and contempt of Connolly and his work. Cyril Connolly always had looked upon Evelyn as his friend, and, while he wrote with restraint on this episode, it was easy to feel the sadness that overwhelmed him.

It brought back to him a picture of Evelyn's 'bloated, puffed-up face . . . with the beady eyes red with wine and anger, his cigar jabbing as he went into the attack'. That is indeed the popular 'image' of Evelyn Waugh, and Cyril Connolly is justified in drawing it, but there was a time before wine and anger had got to work on those eyes, before there was any cigar to jab, when the sheet of paper lying under Evelyn's hand was not liable to find itself disfigured with vindictive distortions.

This, then, is a sketch of Evelyn as he was as a boy and a young man. It is based on diaries, on some material of Evelyn's own, on events, and, of course, on memory which is bound to be fallible and may possibly be biased in favour of the subject on which it is concentrated. But I do not think that this is an idealised impression. Evelyn, when young, was an immensely stimulating companion, generous in mind and of boundless courage and vitality. He had the gift of making everything seem fresh and exciting. He seemed (the qualifying term, alas, insists on its inclusion) to take pleasure in friendship given and to do his utmost to enrich it—the dagger that was to bury itself in the backs of those who thought themselves to be his friends was then but a shadow of a shadow, less palpable by far than that which marshalled Macbeth the way he was to go.

The child was not destined, however, to be the father of the man; or rather, if he was, then the man, as that disastrous book *A Little Learning* showed, was fanatically determined on parricide, on wiping from the earth all memory of the marvellous creature that was Evelyn Waugh when young.

But somehow I do not think that his murderous work was ever quite completed. I believe that even while, for instance, he was engaged in his cruel thrusts at Cyril Connolly, that a part of him, the generous, the responsive, part, the survivor of his past, was watching aghast and with powerless regret what his present self was doing.

His own Diaries, extracts of which were published last year in *The Observer* and which are to appear in full in the future, are not conclusive evidence one way or the other.

What they do show is that Evelyn was capable of adapting his personality to suit the individual with whom he was, at any particular moment, concerned. Thus his addiction to schoolboy smut, and indeed his lifelong, if intermittent, interest in the language of off-beat sexual deviation, is startling, the more so because it was not obtrusive and was not forced on those who were interested in other traits in his character. What is more, when he was with those people, he himself, if he cared for them, enjoyed playing the part they expected of him. 'Playing the Part' is perhaps misleading; in his young days he *became* the person his admirers wanted him to be; there were so many facets to his personality that he could turn the appropriate one to the light without, as it were, playing false to any of the others.

What remains an intractable problem is the paradox that while Evelyn, in the second half of his life, repudiated his comfortable, bourgeois Hampstead and went, packing his bodily, mental and spiritual luggage, to live in a more spacious setting and with the class that inhabited it, he never lost his strong attachment to his past and the friends he made there. He may have been right in feeling that, with his sense of tradition and his love of the forms of gracious living, his adopted country would suit him better than that into which he was born, but why then should he cling, in spirit at any rate, to the friends of his youth he so maligned in both the spoken and the written word?

'I would think that he was always very fond of you', wrote Roger Fulford in a letter dated June, 1973; but there is scanty evidence available, apart from the collection of letters in the United States to which reference is made in a passage on another page, to bear out his opinion. However, both the Diaries and *A Little Learning* are suspect; the latter is filled with distortions and omissions which themselves distort, and the Diaries are a series of puzzles.

It seems to me that Evelyn the diarist set down opinions and records of events which differed profoundly from the activities indulged in by himself and those with him at any given time; indeed, only when he is writing of his experiences on active service can he be said to be entirely objective. Evelyn may have been enjoying himself with those he found congenial, but when he came to set his judgement down, his whole personality seems to shrink and distort itself to the mean outline of a hanging judge. Certainly his friends were shocked and hurt by his opinions of them as set down on paper; the shock was so much the greater because so unexpected.

When Evelyn was not being the hanging judge he allowed himself to be the licensed, the over-licensed, jester. It is a mistake to look into the Diaries in the hope of finding photographic likenesses; that was not at all Evelyn's way. What he was after, always with the idea of capturing more material for his creative writing, was the shock of grotesque and unrealistic, though often highly comic, studies in extravagance. Thus Olivia Plunket Greene is presented in a way in which he never seriously could have thought of her; he has spotlighted a part of her personality which, in a certain set of circumstances and for a limited period of time, might have caused her to behave in a manner which would give him a 'legitimate' platform on which to assemble his effects.

If Evelyn Waugh had in sober fact resembled the monster that sometimes seems to take over the writing of his Diaries and which dictated the course of *A Little Learning*, then the affection in which he was held by a large number of people becomes quite inexplicable; a reading of David Pryce-Jones's book *Evelyn Waugh and His World*, which contains 16 tributes from men and women who knew him, is a salutory corrective to the idea that he had no human qualities to recommend him. Yet the black cap grows more obtrusive, the judgements more bleak and censorious, and the desolating possibility remains that perhaps, after all, what he set down for himself to read was his definite and final word. His friends, who thought they knew how inspiring and considerate he could be, may have been deceiving themselves all along; his more attractive side may have been an illusion, and the cunning artificer of the wounding and denigrating phrase the real man after all. That is a bleak thought. Toward the end of his life the burdens of encroaching age, bad health, insomnia and the first symptoms of what might be called Pinfold's Disease intruded on what might, and should have been, a successful life and further confused the issue. At any rate there was an

Evelyn Waugh who gave and took pleasure in giving and who was a perpetual inspiration and delight. To that Evelyn Waugh this perhaps over-simple book, in which there are elements of narrative, character sketch, and period piece, is a tribute.

Part I

'Oh yes, he fairly rolled out his qualifications, like a maid-servant applying for a post,' wrote Alec Waugh in *The Loom of Youth* in relation to a row between his hero and a games-master who was in the habit of referring to his distinguished career as a player and coach of Rugby football.

This tribute, based on a theory I have of the inner drive and essence of this formidable being that was Evelyn Waugh, is the result of the relationship I established with Evelyn over the years from 1920 to 1931.

This, superficially, is not a statement easy to substantiate since the body of letters written by Evelyn to me during his Oxford years and afterwards are with a transatlantic university and cannot be quoted from. I got rid of them in a spontaneous reaction of hurt resentment at *A Little Learning*; it was childish, but it was natural.

Some things remain, however, and could even direct quotation from his letters have brought the Evelyn Waugh of 1924 any appreciable distance closer to the eyes of a generation which finds even the Evelyn Waugh of, say, 1954, a remote figure, a marionette jerking with conscious eccentricity of movement, against the changing perspectives of history?

What have the quotations from the Diaries so far published done to establish Evelyn as a credible human being? They have assembled the theatrical parts necessary for the erection of an outsize creation, at once frightening and pathetic, with the outraged glare of wide accusing eyes bearing all too close a resemblance to the red nose of the pantomime clown. The background, the props, are all there, but what is there to suggest that, on the obverse side of the coin bearing Evelyn's posed profile against its chosen background of stately homes, there might lurk the features of a Dylan Thomas set against a multitude of inn signs? What to whisper that, instead of being at home in White's, he might, like Bramwell Brönte, have found a second home in The Black Bull? Here the Henry Lamb portrait is significant.

Or where, and more important, in the history of Evelyn Waugh as documented by himself was there that which would imply that the grandiose figure destined to dissolve so tragically into Pinfold had its origins in a boy given to natural affection and generosity? True, the boy is no more 'real' than the heraldic symbol that was ordained to supersede him.

Perhaps that is not fair. There was a 'real' Evelyn perhaps to be found in his role as husband and father, in his devotion to the more conservative elements in the Roman Catholic Church or on the battlefields of Crete serving under a commander to whom he could give his admiration; there was, it is tempting to argue, a 'real' Evelyn in the days before he found it necessary to inflate himself to the proportions appropriate to the part he had chosen to play.

Yet the actor does not become any more 'real' when he sits down in his dressing room and takes off the costume he has been wearing—and, besides, Evelyn was not long in getting to the point when the costume proved impossible to dislodge.

It is, perhaps, then, as well to put down these impressions of Evelyn as I knew him from the years 1920 to 1931 and not to be too concerned with the intricacies of hindsight—and there was certainly enough in the Evelyn of those days to demand, and satisfy, entire attention.

The inside seats on the buses
And the paths across the downs.

This couplet mirrors well enough the nature of our relationship at Lancing and in the years that follow ('If you force me to be Polonius at the age of 18, for God's sake don't turn out to be Laertes,' I remember him saying), for the inside seats on the tops of those open-deck buses we used to take in the holidays, and the paths, affording a level walk as against the steep inclines of the downs on either side of them, were favoured places—and these Evelyn took, not through deliberate arrogance but through an inner conviction that they belonged, as by natural right, to him.

There were, at that time, two strains in Evelyn that were different though not in conflict. One, the natural assumption, not exactly of leadership, not exactly of self-assertion, yet of something in which those two elements were blended. The other was an *acted* ferocity, the bulging, incredulous eyes, the bark of the voice which so intimidated Cecil Beaton in Evelyn's prep-school days—these were assumed to amuse himself, and, if the person at whom this barrage of aggression was directed was amused rather than intimidated, then so much the better and Evelyn joined in the laughter and reverted to his natural self. The trouble is that as he grew in age and reputation, he found all too few people who guessed that his rudeness and apparent intolerance were, in reality, invitations to a game, and when there was, as it were, no one to play with, the mask he was once so willing to discard set into a harsh pattern which could not easily be thrown off. Evelyn referred to his father as a born actor who performed in private life instead of on the stage; Evelyn inherited that particular characteristic.

This is not to deny that there was something inherently thrusting and aggressive about him. It was there in the square, strong body, in the set of the eyes, in the manner of his walk, which somehow suggested that he was always going slightly uphill.

And then, of course, there was his courage, which was fantastic. There was nothing of which he was afraid, and his war record was entirely in character. He was not good at games and not particularly interested in them—he was, however, a reasonable swimmer and boxer. Yet I see him in my mind's eye on a winter's day of mud and rain playing in some kind of house football match against boys older and heavier than himself and ploughing his way along by sheer determination, fighting not so much to get the ball into the net as to demonstrate his indifference to kicks, knocks, and his own lack of ability as a player.

He wore glasses then and, while he could set his rather pale, squarish face into the kind of look which made such an impact on Cecil Beaton, he cultivated a kind of dead-pan expression which so well suited the tone and humour of his prose. There was much of Buster Keaton in Evelyn Waugh—when he was not being the outraged sergeant-major.

One of those 'paths across the downs' led to a cottage rented by Francis Crease, who seemed at first sight a caricature of an old spinster, but who had more to him than that. He helped Evelyn with the illuminated script on which he was then so keen. Evelyn has written of this in this autobiography, but his account is more revealing for its implications than its statements. Evelyn throughout that particular chapter is concerned in comparing Francis Crease with J. F. Roxburgh to the latter's disadvantage, and that is typical of his determination, whether conscious or not, to falsify all that he was, and all that happened to him, during those Lancing years.

In a letter he wrote to me a year or so before he died he said that if I read his book more carefully I would see that he was at pains to emphasise how odious he, Evelyn, was at that period. A disarming piece of self-denigration it would seem, but it simply is not true. He was certainly something of a rebel, a nuisance on occasions to authority, and in his last term or two he was bored with the place, as witness the 'Corpse Club', and impatient to move on to Oxford, but there was much at Lancing to inspire him. And the fount of that inspiration was Roxburgh.

'J.F.', as he was always known and who afterwards became the first headmaster of Stowe, was an unusual master in the strict and unimaginative atmosphere of public school life in the immediate post-war days; although Lancing was, and has remained, in the 'liberal' tradition. 'J.F.' was an elegant man and he dressed like one. He was also a civilised one, and to learn from him was a delight.

He was ready and generous with his appreciation—and no one knew that better than Evelyn. In my diary there is a parody of Landor's epigram which Evelyn wrote in 1921—

I strove with none, for they might strive too well,
Nature I feared, but gently toyed with Art;
I warmed both feet before the fires of hell,
They rise—and it is prudent to depart.

'It's magnificently clever,' I confided to my diary and added: 'J.F. likes it a lot.'

'J.F. likes it a lot'—and he always was ready to express his admiration. Evelyn writes of his Lancing days with a bias against them, but the truth is that he was bursting with ideas and enthusiasms, and, with discrimination from 'J.F.', those ideas and enthusiasms were encouraged. Even Evelyn admits that we intoxicated ourselves with conversations on every subject under the sun; there was then a warmth in Evelyn, an appreciation of the ambitions and problems of others.

When we, and by 'we' I do not mean solely Evelyn and myself, but a number of others, were not talking we were writing, and here it was that Evelyn showed himself at his most generous. I was writing essays or short stories or poems or the beginnings of novels and they all were submitted to Evelyn for his criticism or approval. It may seem absurd now that he and I should have fallen into a master–disciple relation when we were merely schoolboys, but it did not seem like it then.

But then Evelyn was indeed old, although not as sophisticated as he liked to make out, for his age. He worked hard at curing me of my conventionality of mind and inclination toward the more glucose forms of sentimentality. Nothing was too much trouble for him and here are some notes of criticism he wrote on one of my writings:

> Very good. I am proud to see places where I can discern my own influence. I like it immensely
>
> but
>
> (1) Avoid long conversations on general subjects. This is a mistake many people make. A great many of your readers will know far more than you about Nash and Nichols, none of them know anything of Ralf or Rodney. General conversations may only be allowed when they show character.
>
> (2) The style is still too sloppy, particularly at the beginning. Don't be slack about grammar and do quote accurately if you must quote.
>
> (3) For God's sake don't hold up *The Wandering Jew* as a literary or aesthetic show.
>
> (4) Don't put down thoughts at such length. Directly suggest—be subtle, leave something to us readers.

(5) *Keep cutting out*—motto for artists of all sorts. Prune unessentials. Don't describe characters just to bring them in—e.g. 'Praeters'.

N.B. Rodney and Jimmie are quite brilliantly played off together. Peggy is interesting. Father and mother too shadow [*sic*]. Household collectively lacks character, however elaborately described individually —for description of 'household character' see G. B. Stern's *Larry Munro*, a thoroughly unpleasant book, but one family, friends of ours, brilliantly done.

That seems to me remarkable criticism for a boy of 17. It is balanced and self-confident.

He himself, of course, wrote but with more economy and less extravagant dedication. And, as he advised me in my writing, so did he in my reading; the poems he marked in my *Oxford Book of Victorian Verse* throw a revealing light on the bent of his own mind.

Early on, he showed how he valued form. That parody of Landor's sprang from appreciation of the author—and, like many others of his age, he revelled in the ordered pessimism of *The Shropshire Lad*. He had a fondness for the *fin-de-siècle* verse which carried the banner of the *Yellow Book* (it is astonishing, incidentally, that Arthur Waugh, who was everything that periodical was not, contributed to its first number) and, for instance, Richard Middleton's *Pagan Epitaph* and *On a Dead Child* are marked with heavy, approving crosses. Surprisingly, considering Evelyn's indifference to nature and the countryside, Belloc's *The South Country* pleased him and, naturally considering our ages, Ernest Dowson's *Non Sum Qualis Eram* . . . delighted us both. Lionel Johnson fails to get a marking, but Arthur Symons is there with *Emmy*, and a vehemently pencilled approval is given to Richard Le Gallienne's *The Second Crucifixion*, a second-rate religious poem if ever there was one.

On occasions Evelyn and I talked about religion; he inclined then to an agnosticism that trembled on the edge of atheism.

In this context it is important to add that the Chapel at Lancing had a beauty and an atmosphere which insisted on making themselves felt. Music meant nothing to Evelyn, although with Brent-Smith as organist and in charge of the choir, the standard of the musical part of the services was high. It is typical of Evelyn's unexpected approach to things that he insisted that the best way of appreciating the Chapel was not from the inside but by lying down on the grass outside under the building and staring up. And he was right—the stone seemed to soar into the sky and, after a time, it made us almost as giddy as though we had been on the roof looking down.

To return to that book of Victorian verse. 'Q's' *Alma Mater* gets the accolade and so does Oscar Wilde's *Requiescat*. Evelyn's taste, then, was not in any way remarkable, and he himself, in *A Little Learning*, wrote of the mistake he had made by his excessive admiration of the American novelist James Branch Cabell.

. . . . .

The considerable unofficial interest taken in the arts at Lancing at that time had talent to sustain it. The sixth form, after all, had among its numbers apart from Evelyn himself, Hugh Molson, Tom Driberg, Roger Fulford and Max Mallowan ('What a remarkable lot you were,' wrote Roxburgh to me in 1950) and we and others formed a society known as the Dilettanti which indulged in various forms of aesthetic activity, if that is what it can be called.

There was an Art Group, for instance, and we had arranged for a professional artist to judge our sketches—his name was Detmar Blow—and to award a first prize of £2, a handsome sum as things went for schoolboys in

1921. Now Evelyn could draw and paint well. I never quite knew why he dropped his drawing so completely as time went on. It may have been that his days at an art school after Oxford coincided with an unpropitious phase of his life. At any rate, we spent many hours on the downs sketching the view for all the world like two Victorian maiden ladies. Evelyn was well ahead of me and, with that off-hand kind of certainty that was so typical of him, he had made sure in his own mind that the prize was as good as his.

And so it ought to have been, but Detmar Blow divided it between Evelyn and myself. Evelyn's reactions to this were typical. He expected me to acknowledge, which I did, that a miscarriage of justice had occurred, a miscarriage so gross as to defy explanation, but at the same time he was genuinely delighted at my success, and, since he had not the full £2 to spend himself, he made it clear how part at least of my sum should be laid out. 'There's no excuse now, Carey' (the nickname I was known by), 'you can buy that new Cabell novel now,' and he fixed me with that mock ferocious glare which I used to call 'that face'. And so I had to acquire *Jurgen* or *The High Place* or whatever it was, and the most dismal nonsense it seemed to me although I was too loyal to say so.

All this may give the impression that my entire four years at Lancing were spent in Evelyn's company; this, of course, was not so. It was only when we were relatively senior that we became friends and then rigid conventions prevented boys from different houses—and I was not in Evelyn's house—from seeing too much of one another. Thus it was the custom of older boys to walk in the evenings two or three times round the two quadrangles, the Upper and the Lower, in company with another boy of their same age and house.

Now my general gregariousness was a sore trial to

Evelyn, who regarded what he called my lack of reticence with distaste. And so it would sometimes happen that while I and a friend from my own house were walking in one way and discussing Eternity, the poetry of Stephen Phillips or the state of Kent cricket, all subjects equally dear to my heart, we would meet, among the other perambulating couples, Evelyn and, say, Roger Fulford, coming in the other. It was then Evelyn's custom when hearing my voice and, especially if something like Eternity was on the conversational menu, to glare as we passed and say: 'Soul on the hearth-rug, Carey?' and I would answer: 'Oh, Evelyn, that face!' and we would go our respective ways laughing.

. . . . .

But there were occasions when we were together for longer periods than the timetable and the thousand-and-one other pressures of school life allowed. There was at Lancing a system known as Veniam Days, which normally coincided with Saints Days (Lancing was a High Church school) and were, in effect, whole holidays. Boys who had parents or relations in the neighbourhood could take friends out for the day. I remember once going with Evelyn to see Alec, who was then living with his first wife in a cottage at Ditchling, and very impressed I was at my first sight of the author of *The Loom of Youth*, still the best, in the sense of the truest, account of public school life ever written.

It so happened, however, that my mother and step-father lived at Hove, and so it was easier for Evelyn to come home with me on these occasions.

Evelyn's conduct in the face of older people living in a nondescript kind of Hove villa is not without interest. My step-father was the kindest and simplest of men, a member of the Stock Exchange with a golf handicap of 2. He always was hugely amused by my insistence that Evelyn would be a great man and author and by the care with which I hoarded Evelyn's letters and any writings, school essays and so on of his, on which I could get my hands.

My mother was a beautiful woman, but her idea of a good book was Ethel M. Dell's *The Way of an Eagle*. Like my step-father, she laughed at my faith in Evelyn's glorious future, and yet a certain feminine intuition (at least it might have been) made her uneasy with him. I think she sensed in him something arrogant and dangerous; there were moments when she seemed to be treating him like a time-bomb.

All this is hindsight and perhaps a too-imaginative reconstruction of events and attitudes. Outwardly, Evelyn was treated like any other school friend I had invited home for the day and Evelyn, well, it would be easy to write that Evelyn responded in kind. Up to a point he did. His manners were perfect; the trouble was that they were a little too perfect. No one could present such a shining front of courteous innocence as Evelyn when he wanted, and, behind that front and inspiring it, was, of course, irony, or to put it in schoolboy terms, cheek; cheek, pure and simple.

Yet it would not be fair to imply that Evelyn was incapable of enjoying himself in an uncomplicated way or that he did not, in his own fashion, appreciate such breaks in the routine of Lancing life. Certainly we went on the West Pier, put pennies in slot machines and amused ourselves generally. I think my family set-up entertained him in a way my parents did not suspect (at least perhaps my mother did) but that did not prevent him from coming again and expressing his gratitude in terms that had a parody flavour of eighteenth-century elaboration about them.

. . . . .

In writing of the austere routine of Lancing life, there is the danger of underlining the impression Evelyn set out to create in his chapter on the place in *A Little Learning*, an impression of grey monotony and of mediocrity among boys and masters alike. Certainly the discipline would seem monstrous by present-day standards, but it did not seem excessive to us, and there was always Roxburgh—and some other masters as well—to patronise, in the better sense of the word, our interests and enthusiasms. Things were not as grim as Evelyn liked to pretend.

Take, for example, Evelyn's play. He makes no mention of it in his book, although it caused him and a lot of other people a lot of hilarity at the time. It was called *Conversion: The Tragedy of Youth in three burlesques*. Act I was entitled *School, as maiden Aunts think it is*; Act II, *School, as modern authors say it is*, and Act III, *School, as we all know it is*.

Act I was all about tuck boxes and dormitory feasts, and it was in Act II, a parody of his brother's *Loom of Youth*, that Evelyn let himself go and brought the house down. His characters paraded about in First Eleven or house blazers and scarves in a state of hysterical anxiety over a house match to be played on the following day. Some wretched youth ventures to bring up the subject of work to be met with horrified amazement at the very thought that anyone could think of work on the eve of a house match; the nail biting and nervous pacing up and down resume.

It all was written with an extreme competence and certainty of touch, and, once again, Roxburgh was lavish in his praise. Evelyn much appreciated it at the time; it was only afterwards that Roxburgh subtly is cut down to a size that was a caricature of his real stature.

. . . . .

I have forced myself to look through a diary I kept of those Lancing years; Evelyn, of course, was keeping one as well—and a highly idiosyncratic one it has turned out to be, although the whole may tell a different story from the parts that have so far been published. I say forced, because there is something uncomfortable about dragging up records of lost days. It gives an unpleasant feeling of unreality, the diarist and reader of the diary poised awkwardly between the cares and preoccupations of comparative old age and the memories of youth, like passengers on the flimsy saddle of an uncertain Time machine: but the record I kept was an honest one and contains much of what I had forgotten.

What I have remembered and set down so far is, however, confirmed, although I thought it was I who had prophesied that Evelyn would be the Max Beerbohm of his age—that, it appears from an entry dated Saturday, May 21, 1921, was said by his father. My own note on what Evelyn told me his father had said was 'No, Evelyn. You'll be greater. You're a creator.'

Also, judging from another entry on the same date, I seem to have been more advanced in my sketching than I had supposed and to have been capable of criticising Evelyn's efforts.

Saturday, May 21
Another lovely day. Went out with Evelyn this afternoon and talked to him while he sketched. He has done a ripping caricature of his brother, but I don't like his sketches. He regards the pigments merely as a medium and fulfilling no function of their own. They're harsh and not to my taste but they have a definite object. A study of trees he did I liked and am going to do myself. We talked about the futility of most people, a thing I have onlyjust begun to realise. 'You've developed tremendously lately, Carey.'

There follows the remark of Arthur Waugh's and the parody of Landor already quoted and I go on—

> He's a tonic, by Jove he is, and I am frightfully bucked by a remark he made to me at the end when I said how much I had enjoyed myself. 'Don't thank me, Carey. I've enjoyed myself too, awfully. You're one of the very few people whose company I prefer to my own.'

The funny divine idiocy of youth. The whole of that summer of 1921 seems in retrospect a golden bowl of sun, downland and air embracing an innocence which lay quiescent like still water yet sparkling and alive. I stress the innocence—despite Evelyn's unexpected stress on 'filth' in his diaries—because so much of my diary is concerned with my romantic emotions towards a smaller boy. It was a natural and protective relationship and so patently harmless that my housemaster, dear, kind 'Dick' (W. B.) Harris, was at a loss to know how to tackle the problem. It is mentioned only because it occasionally got in the way of my acting as Boswell to Evelyn's Johnson. However, there are entries which run from March 3, 1921, to January 30, 1922.

On Monday, April 4, I went to London (this was the Easter holidays) and saw *The Beggar's Opera* with Evelyn and 'Praeters' (Hugh, now Lord, Molson) and spent the night with Evelyn's parents. There is no elaboration here and the diary, so far as Evelyn is concerned, skips to May 1 when I showed Evelyn a 'lot of painting but not very satisfactory. An interior, two small landscapes, two big landscapes, scene from *Beggar's Opera* and one from *Othello*, and one sea-scape.'

Evelyn delivered his verdict. 'Said *Othello*, *Beggar's Opera* and one big landscape were bad but liked other big landscape rather a lot. Said interior was pleasant but out of drawing. "Still caricaturing Matisse, Carey?" ' This last, incidentally, illustrates the difference in general culture between my own home and Evelyn's. I doubt whether my parents had ever heard of Matisse.

On Thursday, May 12, I record—

> Went down with Evelyn to Shoreham this afternoon. We had a very pleasant time and a nice tea. What an extraordinary person he is . . . he fills me with a sense of my own dignity and the greatness of my soul.
>
> I love the quaint mentality of his brain—his way of branching off and pointing out the beauty of a corner of a house, of a shop-front. 'Study street architecture, Carey.' His affectations. 'There's a delightful squalor about Shoreham.'
>
> If only I could hold his affection I shall be alright. He understands, perhaps he alone. 'Poor Carey. I can understand all your moods, but I can sympathise with this one. Go out by yourself on the downs, walk. When I feel like you, I'll come with you, but I'm sane now. My divine fire's dying. Poor Carey.'
>
> Oh, but he's great. I have got unwavering faith in his genius.

This particular extract shows that my Boswelling was pretty accurate. Diaries are apt to be suspect for the reason that the writer is tempted to fill them, not with events and conversations as they actually happened, but as he would have liked them to have happened. Evelyn's own diaries, to judge from the extracts so far published, are one long exercise in his own particular brand of fantasy. This, however, seems perfectly to mirror the sententiousness of youth, and however odd it may seem considering what is known of Evelyn Waugh as he became, Evelyn was not immune from it. 'My divine fire's dying . . .'—that is the authentic Evelyn as he could be at 17.

I find that I go on with a passage remarkable considering our ages and the general circumstances.

> I wish [I wrote] I could do Evelyn justice. Some day I will try and do a character sketch of him. If anyone should ever read this diary I should like them to say 'He must have been a remarkable character. A wonderful intellect, a deep sympathy and a straight, balanced mind.'
>
> People say he's hard but I know better. 'Not to the strong am I sent but to the weak.' Not to the self-satisfied clever egoists but to a sorrowful, worried me. 'I understand. I've felt like it myself often. Poor Carey.'

Despite the absurd solemnity of the language in which the young of that period sometimes wrote (and, indeed, sometimes spoke), the point is that Evelyn was a person who gave, who interested himself abundantly in the farcical and fanciful woes of those of whom he was fond, who was himself both sensitive and sympathetic. I did not write those words in my diary but I do know that they reflected what I felt at the time, and what I continue to feel.

On the following day, Friday, May 13, I recorded that I had started to read Stephen Phillips' *Paolo and Francesca,* and I added the comment 'Evelyn assures me it has some of the finest love scenes in the English language.'

On Tuesday, May 17, I wrote 'Chatted with Evelyn and "P.F." [Machin] in the library after tea. What a sense of humour he [Evelyn] has got! Also he gave me his poem to read. As far as I've got it is not great, but one cannot be great in Spenserian stanzas.'

The next day I criticised Evelyn—at least to my diary. 'Have just read Evelyn's poem,' I wrote. 'It is awfully good but is spoilt by his having to make rhymes of words which don't fit in. Still this is scarcely his fault. There are some striking bits—

the world is not more sweet
for men's good acting, nor for human pain
more ugly nor more wise for any human brain.
When you had hope you cried "The world is good"
and when your hope proves false you ride alone
and cry "The world is ill" and in this wood
fall down and ask for rest. But I was shown
at night among the reeds and grasses blown
the world is neither good nor bad and rest
abides as much in forest, down and stone
and may be met in crowds. Those are the blest
who find it in themselves and guard it best.'

That seems to me now by no means bad, but I commented that it is 'surely an echo of that great poem in *The Shropshire Lad*—

Therefore since the world has still
much good, but much less good than ill.'

This criticism, added to an entry for Thursday, May 19, 'Evelyn wanted me to go out on the downs for lunch and the afternoon but couldn't as I was playing Leagues' (a form of Lancing house match), indirectly indicates what I have been beginning to suspect since I set my memory working, to suspect, that is, that I was rather more independent in my relationship with Evelyn than I had been inclined to suppose. Certainly I admired him inordinately, as he deserved to be admired, but mine was not a mere doormat role. Indeed it could not by the nature of things have been, for such a relationship would soon have bored and revolted him. Evelyn always wanted someone to stand up to him.

On the next day I 'read the III Act of Evelyn's play. I like it awfully—much better than the 1st. His hero is a rebel fighting against the sound and platitudinous arguments of the Head of his House on the question of discipline and loyalty to institutions. "If you weren't a prefect, Maine, I should call you a prig. You can't realise that anybody can go on doing a thing deliberately without a high principle behind him." '

There followed the sketching day already described and a remark by Evelyn. 'There's a very good chance of your being a really good novelist, Carey,' which was not to prove prophetic. There seemed to have been some kind of school essay competition going on at this time and I see that I gave my entry to Evelyn to read. On Thursday, May 26, I record—

> Evelyn wrote a ripping letter on my essay. He says it's by far the most interesting thing I have ever shown him and demonstrates more clearly than any incident the enormous development I've undergone in the last year. He finished up on a rather personal note which caused great surprise to 'Praeters' who never guessed Evelyn cared for me so much.

The picture so far is certainly of a past age and the colours appropriate to it should be brown and faded. But somehow they are not. They have the brightness and vigour of illustrations in a children's book—instead of dinginess there is light and clarity. Perhaps there always is with youth, but perhaps also there is magic in those particular times, so disillusioning for those a few years older than ourselves, just as there assuredly was in Evelyn.

And so on to the next day, when I noted that I had been reading Arthur Waugh's *Reticence in Literature* and commented 'For the father of Evelyn, Arthur Waugh has eminently sane views'. That was a Wednesday and on the Thursday I wrote:

> Read Act II of Evelyn's play in early school. It's simply gorgeous—the best of the lot I think. The way he rags *The Loom of Youth* is splendid, especially that part where what's-his-name's expelled. 'Before I came to Fernhurst I knew nothing. Fernhurst's taught me all I know and now I contaminate it', or words to that effect. He's ragged that part beautifully. The remark he makes an intellectual who is being ragged make: 'Why can't you chaps leave me alone, you know I'm as immoral as you are?' and the athlete's reply: 'What's the use of being immoral when you're not good at games?' is typical of school as modern novelists would have us believe it is.

On June 3, the next day, the subject of the play is still to the fore.

> I am so pleased. First Meynell [Sir Francis?] wanted to publish Evelyn's play and sort of hawk it round the public schools. As Evelyn says: 'It's very kind of him but I don't think he understands public schools' but now J. C. Squire has asked to see it with a view to publishing it in the *Mercury*.
> Isn't it splendid? I'm so glad, and so is Evelyn and he shows it more than I thought he would, although of course he says it probably won't be taken. Anyhow it's awfully good.

There is not a word of all this in *A Little Learning* but it shows that he was getting a measure of appreciation in the outside world at an early age. I suspect Roxburgh's influence here.

On Sunday, June 5, I

> Went for a walk with Evelyn. He holds I've developed tremendously and changed not for the worse but for the better.
>
> He won't allow that Dick's [my housemaster] creed of social preference is infallible 'the state was created for the individual, not the individual for the state'. Evelyn has come to the realisation of the minuteness of this world compared with the universe and the minuteness of his life compared with the world.
>
> 'You must keep your nose down in the mud, Carey, once you look up, or even forward, you're done. If I thought enough about this I should go mad, you've got to concentrate on your next step and never look beyond.'
>
> He has discovered he is an agnostic but is willing to admit that God probably does exist as a force, like heat or electricity.
>
> 'Religion and emotion help you to concentrate—that's their value.'
>
> Again, 'I am convinced there is no ultimate good or evil. When you take into consideration the immensity of the universe you cannot have the presumption to believe there is. There's a kink in one man's brain which is attracted to what we call good and in another to what we call evil.' I can't agree with this last, nor is the fact of our own insignificance vital to me.
>
> Philosophy like this is a tonic to me but it's hell to Evelyn—he always leaves me wiser and happier.

This 'philosophy' showed that Evelyn was always,

with some part of his mind at any rate, 'interested' in religion. But then, subconsciously or not, Lancing was always at work stimulating the religious impulse. There were many 'sons of the clergy' among the boys, and it was indeed with a religious purpose in mind that Woodard founded the chain of schools of which Lancing was the head. It is almost compulsory to say that boys are put off church or Shakespeare by having them thrust down their throats; it is by no means certain.

It is true that we had a more than generous ration of Chapel, two half-hour services every week-day and two full-scale ones on Sunday, but this was far from being torment. The evening service, in particular, when the body was agreeably tired with exercise, could be a soothing, pleasant thing and it was curious how many unlikely types would stay on for the voluntary—and it was voluntary in the real sense of the word—organ recital after Sunday evensong. We were, what is more, soaked in the language of the Bible, the Book of Common Prayer and the English Hymnal and, while no one would guess it from our behaviour and conversation, I do not believe that it was all without its inward influence.

It was all very well, in other words, for Evelyn to proclaim that the best way of appreciating the Chapel was to lie on his back outside it; the inside of it, and what went on there, was not without importance so far as his thinking and development were concerned. When we were together, however, we were more concerned with out own affairs and on this particular point of religious belief, or the lack of it, he talked more to Tom Driberg than to me, Driberg was then a tall, pale, supercilious, bespectacled youth, extremely clever though not generally popular, but even then he was fascinated by, and learned in, the rituals of the Church and Evelyn realised it and respected him.

Monday, June 6, 'starting to read *The Way of All*

Flesh again' since Evelyn had, most perceptively as it seems now, said that 'he [Samuel Butler] had a derisive brain which could see through himself. He was frightened of himself and *The Way of All Flesh* is the one creative work he left. His others are in the nature of cynical success.'

It is extraordinary how subtle and how misleading to others friendships between young men (for Evelyn and I were now approaching our eighteenth year, an age at which many are now married, and school-boys conjures up a vision of school-caps and satchels) can be. I have never conceived of the word 'jealousy' in connection with the relationship between Evelyn and myself, but it makes an intrusion on Saturday, June 11.

> After lunch took Evelyn down to meet my mother and father [step-father]. They didn't come by the first bus so we had an hour to wait and we wandered along the Lancing road for a bit and that [*sic*] sat down. Evelyn read me a rather sentimental poem dedicated to two boys in his own House in which the lines
>
> But I know that just you two
> Mattered out of all I knew.
>
> Rather disturbing, but the poem is beautifully written. It's rather upsetting all the same. I wonder what Evelyn does think about me.

On Tuesday, June 14:

> Went for a walk with Evelyn at 12.30 down in the dyke-field. I have never known him so cheerful. He was simply bubbling over with spirits.
> In the afternoon Bungy [Roger Fulford] he and I went down to Shoreham and bought strawberries and cream and had tea.

It was awful [*sic*] good fun. Evelyn and I talked poetry and philosophy. Bungy is very conservative and does not get to grips with himself at all.
As Evelyn says 'part of his brain stagnates'.
Of course Bungy accuses me of being a minor addition [*sic*] of Evelyn—well
The man who plants cabbages imitates too, and if I can get further with Evelyn's help than without it, I don't see why I shouldn't like [?] it.
After tea went and sat in the library with Evelyn and made him read *The Hound of Heaven*. It expresses what I sometimes feel and he thought it was great.

It is something of a surprise to find myself advising Evelyn what to read instead of the other way round. I should have thought he would have come across Francis Thompson on his own.

This jealousy business seems to have rankled; it was not, however, jealousy as it might be construed in a modern setting. It was Evelyn's mind I was jealous of and I grudged, and was jealous of, others who deflected it from its concentration on myself and all that was happening to me. I was jealous, in other words, of the *time* he devoted to other things and other people, but there were never any emotional undertones involved. I had spotted Evelyn's genius from the first and I considered, as it were, that I had a vested interest in it.

On Thursday, June 16, I record that I

Walked round and round the cloisters arm-in-arm with Evelyn after Hall at his invitation.
He had heard from his father who says he would be delighted to have me some time next holidays. It is good of them and I am so pleased.
If Bungy can have both Evelyn and I at the same time, I shall go to him [Evelyn] directly afterwards.

> Evelyn thinks it will be an excellent idea if I write and thank him [Arthur] as it will please him awfully so of course I will. I also mentioned the 'just you two' of his poem. He was ripping about it and said that I counted in a rather different way to them, 'an intellectual friendship cemented by personal affection' and called me a silly ass but told me I really did count. This sounds awfully silly but I suppose I am where Evelyn is concerned.

There persists this odd mingling of sophistication, reading *The Hound of Heaven* and so on, with such phrases as 'ripping about it' which should have cried out for ironic inverted commas even in 1921, but apparently it was not so.

On Monday, June 20:

> Evelyn's play came off in the evening. It was simply splendid, a great success . . . Everybody enjoyed it enormously I think. All the masters were there including the Head. I think the Epilogue, which by the way, J.F. remarked 'had a touch of genius in it' is worth reproducing—
>
> If we offend you, in that we have shown
> The faults of others, not disguised our own,
> Say this of us, we merely stand and quote
> The words and sentiments the author wrote,
> And he but drew with undiscerning art
> What laughter taught him, we but learnt the part.
> If he has failed, acquit him of ill-will
> And say in charity, he copied ill,
> He reproduced the shadow, drew the shade
> And blindly copied faults false nature made.
> So for indulgence on his faults we pray
> We stand converted, and so end our play.

On the next day Evelyn took me for a walk and 'told me how pleased he was with the play'—one more example of the way he would react, the most normal reactions to normal pleasures, even if he did suffer from black moods.

On Thursday, June 25, I

Spent all the afternoon with Evelyn, first sitting in the dyke-field, then watching the others, then lying in Gethsemane [a part of the Lancing grounds].

'As long as you *know* you're all right, what does it matter, Carey?'

He also paid me the great compliment of telling me I probably understood him better than anyone else in the school.

'I get depressed, Carey, the people I like never like me; besides its rotten when you think you've got a touch of genius and you don't know how things are going to turn out.'

He encourages me in my hope that I shall be able to write novels.

Evelyn always had a sound appreciation of his own abilities, but he was never conceited. Conceit is a little word implying a little and a common failing, and it is in no way appropriate to Evelyn, then or later. It is curious, incidentally, to come across him echoing the phrase 'a touch of genius' which Roxburgh had used about his Epilogue.

Saturday finds Evelyn philosophising once more.

Went and drew with Evelyn this afternoon in the dyke-field. We talked philosophy and Evelyn enlarged his theory to me that there was no ultimate good.

'Man is governed entirely by his own self-interest,

Carey. Through generations a gradual conviction has come over men that certain things which might be harmful to themselves such as cruelty, murder, etc., are not to be encouraged. That's all.'

My comment on all this was: 'I don't know, I'm sure,' but there was consolation in the news that Mr and Mrs Waugh were coming down for the Brighton match and it was arranged that I should have them to tea.

The tea included, apart from the Waugh's, my own mother and step-father and two step-brothers, to say nothing of Bungy and other friends and my 'pit' (Lancing for study) must have been a crowded place that afternoon. All, then, was sunshine, but the summer of 1921 saw us as senior boys with privilege and prestige.

The early terms were grim enough with the cold—we slept in stone dormitories with the windows open, a minimum of bed-clothes, and then a cold bath when we got up at 6.30. When Evelyn and I first went to Lancing it was still war-time and Evelyn is right in stressing the shabby and second-rate aspect of things. It was not, to be sure, the school's fault that the food was unsatisfactory—actually the authorities did rather well—but there was somehow an impression that the school was pretending to be what it was not. The severity of the beatings, the complicated business of what fifth-form boys could do and wear and what the 'Lower School' could not, these and other things like them suggested that Lancing was imitating a great public school and pretending it was one.

It was not; it was, to use a footballing analogy, near the bottom of the first division (or, to put it another way, among the leaders in the second), but, even in its darkest days, it should have had the sense and confidence to know that it had enough character to be a considerable school in its own right. There was always a special atmosphere about the place.

Not that a small boy breathing an atmosphere of ink and chalk and doing tiresome work at 7.15 on a gaslit winter morning (it may have been electric light; but the impression is of gas) and under the supervision of a bored and disinterested master, could have been expected to speculate on all this, but he did sense that the staff were a scruffy and inefficient lot. On this particular point, Evelyn was justified in running down, and writing off, the place, but the war was the major culprit.

Most of the masters were either too old or for some reason or another did not come up to Service standards, and the results were deplorable. There was no enthusiasm or talent in the teaching and, with some of the more elderly of the masters, there was little pretence of discipline. One classroom presided over by a particularly inept old party was invariably turned into a kind of mixture of snack bar and clubroom where people moved about exchanging gossip and scandal and eating whatever they had managed to buy at the 'Grubber'. Nor was there any protest from authority except an occasional anguished bleat of 'tomatoes I don't mind; sardines I won't have' which epitomised the general demoralisation that had, in 1918, overwhelmed the school.

But the recovery was as swift as it was spectacular. The advent of Roxburgh and the return from the war of young masters like 'Dick' Harris (Evelyn in *A Little Learning* does pay a tribute to 'Dick' which is a little surprising since 'Dick' was at one with my step-father in his amused, tolerant scepticism regarding my faith in Evelyn's glorious future) worked a revolution. The younger boys were freed from that lowering atmosphere of bullying, or something perilously like it, which had hung over their lives.

Their seniors suddenly found an interest in their work and in subjects outside its immediate scope—the very idea of the Dilettanti, that society with its curiosity about the arts which seemed to burst into being of its own accord, would have been unthinkable in 1918. Morale became high and there was an atmosphere of freedom from which Evelyn was not the only one to benefit. A nature such as his was at the time energetic, effervescent, powerful, needed encouragement, and encouragement was what it got.

The remaining bits of the diary covering the summer term of 1921 and dealing directly with Evelyn are rather more sketchy—no more philosophising, it appears. I see that, when the Waugh parents were at that crowded tea party, it was arranged that I should go and stay with them 'about the 14th August', and generally reports run to this same brevity. Thus I will write just 'Evelyn was there' in reference to some school occasion or another, and once, on July 10, I mention that I 'spent the morning with Evelyn first walking round the cloisters with him' and then after Sunday lesson sitting with him in the library when Hill* 'was present for a bit' and then follows the disappointing comment 'it was too hot to talk much'.

On an earlier day, July 5, however, I had 'sat with Evelyn in the library this evening and read Chesterton's *Wine, Water and Song*. They're rather splendid'. But whether Evelyn agreed with this judgement is not clear.

On Saturday, July 9, however, there occurred an incident of some importance in the light of Evelyn's autobiography, for I met Francis Crease. I do not believe that, outside the strict limitations of the illuminated

* J. L. Hill, incidentally, and I had poems included in an anthology called *Public School Verse 1921–22*; there were some distinguished contributors that year, Peter Quennell, Graham Greene, Christopher Isherwood and A. L. Rowse among them.

script business, that Crease had quite the influence on Evelyn he likes to make out, but he certainly made a bizarre and colourful contrast to the grey stone of school life—and Evelyn always delighted in that particular aspect of things. At any rate I record that

> Evelyn introduced me to him. I talked to him for five minutes or so.
> I simply cannot describe him. His gait is mincing, his voice affected and insinuating, his face sharp and almost ascetic. I am going to have tea with him on Saturday and I must own I am rather looking forward to it.

Well, Saturday came and I set down that it was

> quite a memorable day in so much that I went to tea with Crease. I had a pleasant walk and arrived about 2.50. He welcomed me profusely, but at the moment I cannot give any adequate idea of him, of his high-pitched, affected voice, of his nervousness, either real or assumed, of the extraordinary force of some of his remarks and the futility of some others.

Doubtless they were not as futile as I then supposed, but this whole incident baffles me. I remember going to Crease's cottage two or three times but with Evelyn, and I would sit while Crease taught him how to write a particular script (and incidentally changed his style) but why I should go alone I cannot conceive.

Obviously Evelyn asked Crease to ask me and I can only suppose that the thought of this exotic and eccentric person having tea alone with a boy as conventional as I was amused him. I expect he considered it part of my education, which at this particular period of his life, was a full-time job for Evelyn. It had advantages for him too; he could try out his ideas on me and argue with me as with some admiring yet cautious and careful part of himself, not that there was ever much of that.

There is, incidentally, a consideration here concerning Evelyn's own account of Crease. If he discerned, as he implies in *A Little Learning*, that Crease was something altogether out of the ordinary as an aesthete and a scholar without any orthodox qualifications, then that reinforces the impression that Evelyn himself was altogether out of the ordinary as a schoolboy. I saw only the unconventional clothes, heard only the affected, mincing voice of Crease; he saw deeper.

Or did he? Because I know that some passages in that autobiography are distorted, the clear, unequivocating black-and-white of the printed page itself becomes blurred and reveals what I believe Evelyn is saying rather than what the prose seems with such clarity to proclaim. Thus he is indeed generous in his pretentions of gratitude to Roxburgh, yet behind the impeccable phrases, there is a hidden hand at work, tilting with oh, such delicacy and subtlety, the balance against one to whom he owed so much, in favour of an odd, gifted and unhappy man—and not, in the last analysis, to pay tribute to that man so much as to denigrate the other.

Certainly Evelyn was fascinated by Francis Crease and did indeed, as it were, sit at his feet, but some of the charm Crease had for Evelyn lay in the fact that he was not part of Lancing life, and that charm grew with the writing of *A Little Learning* and of hindsight.

One thing more about Crease. It may well have been that the strain of religious mysticism in him somehow transferred something of itself to Evelyn, not normally at that time a person to be associated with such things, to run deep and undetected within him and finally to propel him, as perhaps Olivia Plunket Greene did, along the road of his conversion to Roman Catholicism. If that is so, then Francis Crease did indeed play a key role in Evelyn's life.

Meanwhile there were the holidays and that visit to the Waugh's. Monday, August 15, was spent at the Oval watching the final Test Match between England and Australia and I

> got to the Waughs about 7 o'clock to find that Alec had been to the Test Match also. They were all very kind but Alec has an extraordinary [*sic*] chilling and repressing influence. Directly he comes in Arthur stops making jokes, Evelyn stops being clever, I stop talking and only Mrs W. is left undisturbed. He has gimlety eyes, a baleful glare which unlike Evelyn's is quite unconscious and a big dome-like forehead and a rather quick almost nervous way of speaking. A personality.

On the next day, Tuesday, August 16,

> in the afternoon Evelyn and I went for a successful row on the Regent Canal and on landing were met by Mrs W. and Sylvia Gosse who turned out to be quite an ordinary looking, middle-aged woman. In the evening Arthur read *Evelyn Hope* and some Dowson to us (Alec having returned to Ditchling). He is a little dramatic and somehow I like it.

Then, on Wednesday,

> Evelyn and I went to *The Playboy of the Western World* in the pit. A jolly good play and fine acting. We were awfully amused by the remarks of two young men behind us who after they had delivered a running fire of criticism at every novelist they could think of just got on to Alec as the curtain went up.

I hope they were going to say something complimentary, for, although the relationship between Evelyn and Alec was not close, so far as brotherly relations go, yet Evelyn in his own way respected Alec. There was, of course, the gulf of the War between them, yet Alec was an important part of the Waugh family and both brothers had pride in that family, although there were rifts and stresses within it, both below and, on occasions, above the surface.

On the Friday, Evelyn and I went 'to *Abraham Lincoln*. When Lincoln first came on we thought we were in for an awful evening, but he gradually grew on us till in the end we admired him. The play was ruined by the Choruses.'

On the Sunday,

> Went to a very High Church at Golders Green with Waugh family. Met an old Wykehamist called Bobbie Shaw whom Alec hates, Evelyn likes and Arthur tolerates, who is madly in love with Ursula Kendall, an old love of Evelyn's and a remarkably pretty girl (so I've been told) . . .

Ursula Kendall was the daughter of Guy Kendall who was, I believe, headmaster of University College School. The interest of this extract, however, lies in the fact that there is the mention of a girl in it; and this is something rare. I cannot remember Evelyn and I ever talking much about girls, first, because it was not 'the thing to do', as we understood the phrase, and secondly because, so far as I knew, it was not a subject that attracted Evelyn. He was equivocal and uncertain in his attitude towards sex at this time—his normal, positive forcefulness refused to operate in this particular field.

I remember that on my twenty-first birthday party, which took place on a Thames launch, one of the people

I asked was a girl called Rachel Mayne. She had strikingly good looks and a highly developed mind—Evelyn, in his diary, records that she made an impression on him, although he misspells her name. She was head girl at Bedales at the same time as Malcolm MacDonald was head boy, and I had long been in love with her—her brother was at my prep. school. She was, a young left-wing intellectual, a type equally alien to Evelyn and myself. Nevertheless there was something exceptional about Rachel; Evelyn saw it and was attracted.

There was no sequel to this one meeting and I expect that Evelyn forgot all about Rachel in a month or two, but for the first few times we met after that birthday party, he would ask about Rachel and whether I had seen her. There was nothing particularly notable in this except in the *way* he asked. Usually Evelyn was firing on all the cylinders of his personality, but when he asked about Rachel he became quiet and indrawn as though he were carrying on some complex debate within himself.

This was about the time when Evelyn was involved at Oxford in a friendship which was of emotional importance to him and a cause of some disturbance. He was off his balance at that time, and I think Rachel set him wondering whether he ever would achieve a normal relationship with a woman. Anyway, the time of boyhood ties and friendships was nearly over—Rachel was making her own way in the world and I was seeing less and less of Evelyn and so nothing remains but a clear memory of Evelyn's serious, intent face as he asked me whether I had seen anything of Rachel Mayne.

To continue with that Sunday in August, 1921. It seems that I went out in the afternoon to see some of my own friends and that on arriving home [at Underhill, that is] I found all out but Ernest Rhys and daughter waiting for them. Rhys is a very old man, at least he looks it, while the daughter, Sylvia, 18, is ugly but has glorious red hair and talks sensibly. I should think was jolly nice. So entertained them with great success until the family returned.

Two days later—

In the morning I looked at all Evelyn's old stories and drawings down from the age of five onwards. Although I wasn't particularly struck at the time, I realise now, when I remember what sort of things I used to write at about eleven how good and even striking they are. The war seemed to play a large part in his imagination. Previous to this I had read a long poem, bound by some admiring grown-up called *The World to Come* which was written during his religious craze which had one awfully good descriptive passage of a dark tower.

All memory of these writings of Evelyn's has vanished completely. I am surprised at my reference to his interest in the war but then the writings in question were, of course, done while it was actually in progress.

On Thursday, August 25:

Evelyn left yesterday to go down to Kent to read with 'Praeters' and I went [home, that is] today. As I passed Lords it was Middlesex 160–7.
Without exaggeration it is by far the nicest house I have ever stayed in or that I can imagine ever staying in. The whole atmosphere is simply splendid and there is a kind of naturalness which one would

have thought almost impossible outside one's own house.

Then again both Mr and Mrs Waugh are incredibly nice and Alec although frightening is really very charming. The books and rooms are in just perfect taste and I can truthfully say I've never enjoyed myself anywhere else half so much and I think I made one complete conquest—Arthur.

This, naturally, is altogether too idyllic a picture, but it was a pleasant house none the less and Evelyn could be happy in it.

Part II

My diary starts again on September 3, 1921, and covers the winter term, which was Evelyn's last at Lancing. There is a shift of emphasis in it—the spaciousness of that summer when the air seemed drenched with the idyllic poetry of the late nineteenth century, with, perhaps, a touch of its decadence, seems to contract as the winter shut us more into our respective Houses and their concerns. Certainly Evelyn was bored and impatient to move on, and I saw less of him.

My first mention of him is on Thursday, September 29—

> By the way [I wrote] I forgot to mention that last night there was a meeting of the Debate Committee and it was decided to close the Society. Evelyn, 'Praeters' says, was insufferable because I wanted to know the reasons and thinking it over I came to the conclusion he was too and seeing him this morning I told him so. He said he didn't think he was and said, 'Poor Carey' so of course I forgave him.

Then nothing but extracts about House politics, football, fives and reading, independent, it would appear, of Evelyn's advice, until Sunday, October 16:

> In the afternoon I went out with Evelyn. He is very 'edgy' and gets irritable especially with . . . We both came to the conclusion that the term was getting on

our nerves and we formed a B.S.A. (Bored Stiff Association). He has also asked me to stay with him next holidays for as long as I like, an invitation I think I shall accept.

On Saturday, October 22, 'the B.S.A. has matured greatly during the week owing to the energy of Evelyn and it is now known as the Corpse Club and has a membership of 7—very exclusive'.

The next day:

By the way a few days ago I wrote a poem, which I thought had some slight merit, on the Chapel and showed it to Evelyn. I got back a letter which stated in no qualified terms that it was thoroughly bad from beginning to end—'not a single phrase of any value' and with this little addition 'five weeks in the Gibbs House are not good for you. You have forgotten both your friends and poetry. I am sorry to say so, but you are an intellectual chameleon'. (I added the comment, 'I'm afraid it's very true.')

I see that an inaugural meeting of the Corpse Club was held and that two 'spiritual presences' were added to the list of members, the second grave-digger in *Hamlet* and Jehoiachim. The level of schoolboy humour implicit in this does not seem altogether despicable.

On Friday, October 28, I entered the following—'Evelyn's eighteenth birthday, I sent him a letter by the Porter's Lodge which unfortunately he didn't get.' This is puzzling since I can't imagine why I didn't give it to him myself. But, as I have written, the winter term tended to isolate us in our own Houses, and Evelyn was not the only one to feel bored and restless. I failed to win that Essay Prize—Hugh Molson got it—and I wrote ungrammatically in my diary that 'after all compared with the arid desert of this term, the excitements of last term, slightly hysterical though it may have been, was infinitely preferable'.

On Saturday, October 29, there is a vivid entry:

> Went for a tearing walk with Evelyn at 12.30 down in the valley and got thoroughly ticked off. I told him I had just read *Prelude*.
>
> 'Of all the sickly sentimental books I've ever read: it makes me simply furious. That wicked boy with his one pure friendship guarding it like a beautiful white flower. My God, I suppose you imagine yourself like that. Been pouring out your soul on the hearth-rug again? My God, nobody can see through your wretched little soul except me. Weak tea and cold buttered toast, my God' and round went that beastly stick (a heavy, carved affair of which Evelyn was inordinately fond) again.
>
> I simply shrieked with laughter, I couldn't help it. Evelyn keeping up a stream of invective and dashing up the slope at a terrific pace with me alternately trotting, walking, laughing and protesting at his side.

The vision of Evelyn, his carved stick cleaving the air as we dashed up the slopes of the valley on the edge of collapse through laughter and shouting comes clearly to me from that late October morning.

Then again, on November 12, there is what appears to have been a repeat performance—

> I went for a walk with Evelyn in the evening (5.15) and he kept up a running fire of invective as we dashed across the Upper–Lower fields. I got quite hysterical at the caricatures he drew of my letters and we arrived back at 6 o'clock warm, laughing

and exhausted. It's a long time since I've seen Evelyn so cheery.

A day or two later, on November 16, Evelyn was still inclined to cheerful invective, this time at the expense of a poem I had given him to read.

Evelyn gave me his criticism this morning. 'Of course it isn't a sonnet at all . . . as a piece of verse I like it very much . . . It is full of good stuff . . . do make your lines scan . . . the last two lines would be excellent if they had any technical merits at all to help them.'

I see that on Tuesday, November 22, I make the brief entry 'No sign from Evelyn' and then on Sunday, the 27—

After Hall I went for a walk with Evelyn to Coombs and beyond. He was in great form. 'What a terrific power words have, Carey, just words. "And so he giveth his beloved sleep"—that's been running in my head for days, it is not great in itself, there's nothing very wonderful about it, but it just gives me intense pleasure.' Funny because I've been saying those words to myself lately. I do hope he gets his Scholarship—I'm going to stay with him if he does.

This last sentence is a reminder that both Evelyn and I were doing some hard work and reading and the general tone of the November extracts does not altogether bear out Evelyn's own gloomy picture of himself. Certainly he was straining to get to Oxford, but the term was not without its hilarious moments. And then on December 1 I noted: 'Evelyn and Molson went off home today for a weekend's rest before their Scholarship on

Tuesday. Good luck to them. Evelyn was in the best of spirits.'

There was not much left of Lancing life for Evelyn and what there was seems to have been cheerful enough. By Sunday, December 11, Evelyn was back and I had tea with him at his House (Heads). 'Evelyn was awfully bucked and considers he has done as well as ever he will do.' Toward the very end of the term, on Thursday, December 15, there is the following entry:

> A really excellent day. It started off at breakfast with the news that Evelyn got a £100 a year scholarship at Hertford for 5 years.
> I am most frightfully pleased as he has so thoroughly deserved it and I for one always believed he would get it.
> He is awfully bucked and makes no attempt to hide it, it is altogether splendid.
> I wrote to Arthur Waugh congratulating him.
> After vainly searching for some time I found Evelyn in the God-box [Lancing slang for chapel] and we went for a walk round the Lower Field. He was just unfeignedly glad he's leaving, and unfeignedly glad he's got his scholarship—altogether a more 'ordinary' last walk we couldn't have had.

The Lancing extracts come to an end, so far as Evelyn is concerned, with a comment on the last day of term. 'I've seen little of Evelyn but we understand each other just as well. Since he's got his scholarship I'm spending 10 days with him next holidays but I can't "sum him up".'

. . . . .

There are two extracts from diary left and, although they belong to London and not to Lancing, it would be more convenient to give them now. On December 28, I record that I had a letter from Evelyn which 'was illegible but he can't have me to stay which is a pity'. Saturday, January 7, however, I spent:

> all day at the Waughs . . . Alec was at home just finishing *The Lonely Unicorn* which is to be published in the Spring, the first of a trilogy. Evelyn likes it. Evelyn and I went to the British Museum in the afternoon and then back to tea.
>
> Arthur and Mrs W. were as charming as usual and Evelyn the same as ever. He let me read some of his earlier diaries—most engaging documents—full of reference to House-matches [word illegible] etc.

Then again on Tuesday, January 10, 1922:

> Met P.F. [Machin] and Evelyn to lunch. We went to the Spanish Restaurant and had a wonderful omelette and rather a nasty Spanish dish to follow. Then on to the Coliseum. Bransby Williams was terrible. The 1st sketch he did [word illegible], the 2nd, Grock I think over-rated and Cyril Maude rather disappointing, but then he didn't have a chance. I never do like the Coliseum. I think Evelyn was a little annoyed.

And that is the end so far as this part of the diary is concerned.

The next part dealing with the Lancing spring term of 1922 is of less interest since Evelyn had left for Oxford, but there are some extracts for April when I saw the Waughs at Underhill and then a week in May when I went to Oxford to take my scholarship examination and was with Evelyn a good deal of that time.

In my account of the first day of that spring term I write 'I know I shall miss Evelyn horribly'. Evelyn might seem to be too formidable, too alarming, too much, perhaps, of a bully, to possess the quality of 'missability', but to his friends, even in his most difficult times, he was always a person most sorely to be missed when he was not there. He left his own particular vacuum, and no one else could fill it.

There are records of various letters from him and he continued to take an interest in the school magazine which I then was editing. The *Lancing Magazine*, although it was never anything like *The Salopian*, which, in the present generation, was a major influence in the development of *Private Eye*, was nevertheless turned by Evelyn* and to a less degree myself, into something more than a record of school and house matches.

It gave us both a lot of amusement, although masters and Old Boys were scandalised by the iconoclastic tone of our editorials and our disguised contributions to the correspondence columns. A letter from one Old Boy, who seems to have had a sense of humour, has somehow survived:

> . . . Old Boys, who helped to make the Empire (apparently) pouring out floods of indignant bombast about matters which they show clearly enough they do not understand in the least, present members of the School who wish to mar it (apparently) taking a gloomy pride in their cadaverous views, athletes, soldiers, scholars and Scargills all indulging in the fiercest invective at each other's expense, constitute an example of hysterical futility which it would be hard indeed to improve upon.

Lavernia Scargill was one of Evelyn's pseudonyms derived from the lines (Wordsworth's?):

* He was Editor in the winter term of 1921 and I took over from him in the spring.

. . . heard upon Lavernia
Scargill's rustling pines,

'Hopeful', as he signs himself, goes on:

I have been looking through some back numbers of the magazine and I am struck by the gentility of their tone. The hottest controversy centred round the question of tennis courts, the most daring Editorial protested against the rush of events of the Easter Term.

Surely you have fluttered the dove-cotes of the Old Boys sufficiently. Is it fair to egg them on to further absurdities . . .

As for 'Corpse' and his friends, restrain their enthusiasm for mental gymnastics—the mature mind has naturally lost some of its youthful agility and cannot be expected to appreciate them. Let the last three numbers of your magazine be buried in decent obscurity and let us see in the next number an Editorial which deals with Editorial pens, the downs and gentle readers . . .

Evelyn put quite a lot of concentrated effort into the task of turning the school magazine on its head, and from Oxford he wrote me a 'Lavernia Scargill' letter.

Dear Sir,

I remember last term that my old friend 'Corpse' and I were looking over the MS. of the Magazine which the Editor [all three people, 'Corpse', 'I' and the Editor, were Evelyn] and as we viewed the tedious and self-assured letters which converged from all parts of the Empire we resolved that when we had left, *we* would not write letters to the Magazine; no humour, we thought, could be more cadaverous, no pomp more funereal, than that of the O.L. trying to restore the School to the high position it had attained in his day. Well, sir, 'Corpse' has left (he tells me he is very happy now so it can't have been entirely his own morbidity) and the Editor has left and I have left, and now after a few weeks I find myself breaking my vow and writing to you in defence of the more conscientious and now slumbersomely contented 'Corpse'.

I am prepared to believe, sir, that your accomplished correspondent is all that he claims to be in athletics and militarism, but I venture to doubt his claims to scholarship. After all, stripped of its offensive bombast his argument appears to be this.

(a) 'Corpse' says he is discontented and that his friends are too; he thinks it is because of this, that and the other. I can tell him what it is—it is he and his friends that are discontented, not this that and the other.

(b) 'Corpse' says he is discontented, he finds he has no healthy enthusiasm, he thinks he wants this that and the other. I can tell him what he wants, he wants contentment and healthy enthusiasm.

Well I dare say he does—in fact 'Corpse' said that too. One can picture athlete, soldier and scholar saying to a beggar, 'No, my man, you're not starving because you can't work—it's because you don't eat enough.'

I am not sure that a little introspection might not be good for the controversial style of your correspondent. But if his remarks are intended to provoke mirth, surely the school magazine which I know is read by other than O.L.'s (I am glad he realises this —so few O.L.s do) is not the proper place for such grave humour.

Faithfully and sincerely yours,
Lavernia Scargill.

Not exactly a letter of scintillating brilliance, but it shows, as Tom Driberg agrees, that Evelyn still took an interest in Lancing even after he had left it.

When I too had left after that spring term, during which I had so much missed the stimulus of Evelyn's company, I seem to have come up to London early in the holidays, and on Monday, April 24, 'I called at Evelyn's for a moment and found Hugh Molson there. We had lunch at the Old Bull and Bush', and on the next day I

> went up to have lunch with the Waughs. Alec alone was in so I talked cricket in his room for a time. Both Hugh [Molson] and Evelyn were much the same I think.
> After lunch we dashed off to the Alhambra, an indifferent show—and then back to tea. Only saw Arthur for a minute or so as I was going back.
> I was very disappointed at Molson being there as I had wanted to talk to Evelyn about things but of course had no chance.

So much for these glimpses of Evelyn, a figure by a turn of the stereoscopic screw, transported across the gulf of the years, but passive, as it were, observed momentarily in the act of being and then receding again. And so will it be with the record of the week at Oxford although there are times then when he makes some positive assertion, takes an attitude which helps to fill in the outline of the complete portrait which has yet to be accomplished.

On Monday, May 1, I

> caught the 10.45 up. Felt rather 'wind-uppy' but luckily met Evelyn in the High and went back with him to Hertford. After lunch Mallowan [now Sir

Max] and another lad from New College called Beadle called in and we all went down to the river and got into a punt. Immediately it started to pelt, and I got back to the Mitre simply soaked.

The next day I began the exam in Christ Church Hall and then

Evelyn gave a luncheon party consisting of himself, Molson, Mallowan, Hill (and two or three more). After lunch we all went up the river in Mallowan's punt. S . . . got ragged rather a lot over his 'homosexuality' which they all say is terrible. Evelyn went ashore and we went on without him and then we couldn't find him which rather troubled us but he turned up while we were having tea.
Evelyn came to dinner with me at the Mitre and we talked of many things . . . Anyhow he seems to have become much happier and more light-hearted. 'One never worries about anything at Oxford, Carey.'

That word 'homosexuality' is a shock not in itself but it is surprising that it found its way into this diary. I would have been prepared to swear that at that time I had never even heard of it. This may seem curious coming from one who had just spent four years at a public school, yet it was possible then, as I presume it would not be now, to maintain a complete innocence over that time. Certainly my ridiculous infatuation for a small boy was innocence itself, a pale, pallid exaggeration of Pre-Raphaelite romanticism—and with Pre-Raphaelite romanticism the young Evelyn had a surprising sympathy. Evelyn certainly did not share my innocence on this particular matter and, on occasions, the impatient, mocking, iconoclastic side of his nature would assert itself, yet the subject he chose for his first book was

Rossetti, and he had not, even at this time, entirely shed the influences of his father's house.

After that Mitre dinner I note that 'we went to a lecture on "Empire Defence" by Lord Stamfordinham [*sic*]. Die-hard Tory stuff—Toryism is one of Evelyn's new affectations.'

Affectation is the right word, for Evelyn's interest in politics was superficial, to put it at its highest. But just as the young men of the Thirties were inclined by the seriousness of their natures to the Left, so most of us who had missed the war, were tilted by our indifference to 'issues' and a natural frivolity towards the Right. Not that we thought of it in that way—it was simply that there was an inborn bias in our way of looking at things that went well enough with the conception of the traditions of Toryism.

On the next day, Wednesday, in the intervals of doing 'papers' in the Hall at Christ Church, I had lunch with Evelyn, and then in the evening I went to a party given by J. L. Hill. I noted 'Evelyn got drunk pretty quickly . . . but Hill and I remained sober 'though I must say I was feeling very happy. Evelyn is very happy when he is drunk'.

I think Evelyn was happy in his earlier times at Oxford and it was only later that the pressures of drink, lack of money (that was always inevitable given the kind of life he was determined to live and the kind of friends he made), an important emotional disturbance, and his frenzied attack on the social ladder, drove him temporarily into a near-desperate state of mind.

Then on Thursday before I did the History 'paper' I went out with Evelyn and 'he bought 2 vols. of Keats, very nice, Florence Press 18/–. We went round to his book-binders and he had *The Shropshire Lad* bound. His books make me very jealous. After lunch we went to

Iffley Church and then back along the river and saw the eights practising.'

After tea 'we [I am not sure now who 'we' were] went round to Evelyn's rooms and discussed God's sense of humour. Hill, Evelyn and I dined out and then Hill went back and Evelyn and I went on to the Union. I couldn't get in though and went back to Hill's . . .'

The next day was my last and Evelyn seems to have gone out of his way to make things enjoyable for me.

> Had lunch with Evelyn and then coffee with Max. Tea with Evelyn and Molson and then Evelyn took me to the station, leaving me with characteristic abruptness. 'Take things as they come. That is the lesson of Oxford. Nothing matters at Oxford. One mustn't do anything either. Just let things come . . .'

Evelyn was a romantic still, but that particular era for him was coming towards its close. I saw him at Oxford afterwards, and at Underhill, of course, while he was still 'up' and the signs of change were evident. But then that may have been simply due to the fact that I no longer knew so much about him. There were always some things I never knew about Evelyn, although, up to this point, there had been few things he did not know about me. Perhaps leaving me at the station with 'characteristic abruptness'—and abruptness of movement was indeed a characteristic of his—had symbolic overtones.

And so on to the 'inside seats of the buses' part which presents difficulties since the documentary evidence for its existence is, to all intents and purposes, non-existent. My relationship with Evelyn never had the regularity of a straight line such as Mrs Frances Donaldson drew in her *Portrait of a Country Gentleman*, an admirable study in the Academic tradition. Mine is a thing of bits and pieces, the pieces intense and sharply shaped, but there was much missing. The fact that Evelyn went to Oxford and I did not was naturally responsible for a vacuum, although in his early days there, when he was poor and inclined to be lonely, we were close enough.

It was the shattering discovery—although why it was such a shock is difficult to imagine—that he was born neither a member of the aristocracy nor of the landed gentry that blew a large hole in what had been a close relationship. If Evelyn had been told that he was illegitimate and that his father had been hanged, the effect of the discovery that some of his Oxford contemporaries moved in social circles of which he had hitherto known little could hardly have been greater.

He set about a task which would seem impossible, that of re-orientating his whole way of life and of looking at things, with an intensity that was frightening in its dedication. In the early stages of that struggle, in the middle to late Oxford period, that is, and in the years immediately afterwards, he won an astonishing amount of ground but even he could not shake himself entirely free of his background and the people who were part of it.

He was still dependent, in other words, on Underhill. It was his base camp, however much he might despise it, and in charge there was Arthur—his nickname 'Chapman and Hall' was pronounced a good deal more affectionately by his Oxford friends than by Evelyn himself. Then his devotion to his mother still held fast, and Evelyn indeed found himself more tied to Underhill and its associations than he cared. I was part of the Lancing scene, which he repudiated, and part of the Underhill scene which he wished to repudiate and could not, and, because he could not, there came a few unexpected reinforcements to the dwindling army of pieces that made up the jig-saw pattern of our relationship. It survived in a precarious manner until 1928, when he was to have been my best man except that my in-laws-to-be, the Gambles (he was the Dean of Exeter), knew the Fulfords and so Roger, next to Evelyn my best friend at Lancing, stood by me in the Cathedral, and indeed until 1931 when I was living in his flat in Canonbury Square. Evelyn was then elsewhere and both our marriages had broken down.

In those desperate days of trying, with what ultimate damage to himself it is difficult to judge, violently to change his nature and his ambitions to fit the end he had so heroically willed for himself, lack of money was a handicap that made itself everywhere apparent. If the fact that he was dependent on Arthur irked Evelyn, it had in its turn its effect on even Arthur's good nature. Parts of a letter Arthur wrote to me for my 21st birthday are pertinent. 'With all my heart I wish you all good things; what is more I am confident that you will attain them. You are not afraid of work and you realise that without work there are no prizes. You do not despise the things that matter, or speak cynically of character . . .' The letter may have been written to me, but it is obvious who Arthur had in mind while he was writing that particular part.

Underhill, then, represented a way of life in which Evelyn was brought up and which found itself in such violent and unsought warfare with all that he intended to be.

The very scale of the breach between them is an indication that what Evelyn sought to rid himself of—and eventually succeeded in doing so—had established roots deep within him and had, indeed, given him nourishment in the days before the strange and unnatural revolution in his character and way of thinking took place. Underhill was a comforting, and comfortable, household and the stories belonging to it underline and reinforce the impression.

Here are two belonging to Lancing days. Certainly Evelyn and I were still very young. We were going to see John Drinkwater's *Abraham Lincoln* (I think it was the first night at the Lyric, Hammersmith) and as I was wrestling with the work of tying my black tie, Mrs Waugh came in to see if I had everything I wanted. 'Oh, yes, Mrs Waugh, but I cannot tie this wretched thing, it will go all lop-sided.'

Mrs Waugh, always most capable in everything she did, tied it. 'Neither can Evelyn tie his,' she said, and then she added, 'But don't tell him I told you.'

She was not altogether joking, for although Evelyn did not then show an excessive interest in clothes, both of us knew that he would not appreciate a joke about his inability to tie an evening tie properly. He had a strong sense of propriety, and this sense was destined in time to caricature itself.

The other story shows the obverse side of the medal, of his willingness, to laugh at himself, to drop the assumed mask of outraged ferocity, and to share that amusement which, nine times out of ten in those days, was the object of the acted exercise in frightfulness. We were travelling back to Golders Green, the nearest station to Underhill which was almost exactly half-way up the long road to Hampstead, and when we got out, Evelyn took me across to a little newsagent's shop opposite. He had, he said, something important to get, something I, too, must get and read.

This important thing turned out to be a copy of *John O'London's Weekly*, which had just started its life at that time. I had tried this particular paper and had not thought much of it. I told Evelyn so and added that I was surprised that he should be so impressed by it. For a moment or two he turned on the bulging eye, ferocious stare treatment, and then, as suddenly, dropped it. He murmured something to the effect that I might well be right and we walked amiably up the hill to his home.

Another incident underlines the fact that he could be surprisingly amenable. On one of our walks in the evening over Hampstead Heath, we came across a character called the 'Major', who was a friend of Arthur Waugh's, as indeed he was of everyone who knew him. He was the kindest and most endearing of men, only he had a passion for cricket (he was a member of Jack Squire's team, 'The Invalids') and this irritated Evelyn beyond endurance. The 'Major' bored Evelyn, and Evelyn showed it. On that particular evening he began muttering under his breath as soon as he saw who it was looming up in the twilight. His manner to the poor 'Major' was offensive, and I said so. He took the charge with placidity. He merely said that he had enough cricket from his father, Alec and myself without the 'Major' joining in.

The exact words of that few minutes' conversation on Hampstead Heath 50 years ago cannot of course be accurately reproduced now, but that is the general outline of it. It shows a side of Evelyn that has become so overlaid by the legends that have grown up round his character that there is danger of forgetting that it ever existed. Actually, Evelyn as a young man was open to argument and could be remarkably placid, even meek, in the face of opposition. Not always, but sometimes. Sometimes, again, the meekness was another of his masks assumed to amuse himself and, he hoped, his companion, but, again, sometimes, not always.

The house, Underhill, was a comfortable, middle-class home, with the advantage of a garden, reached by a flight of steps down from Arthur Waugh's study, which was of respectable size for London and which Mrs Waugh tended with devotion. Kate Waugh was a remarkable woman without in any way appearing so. She was slim and wiry, with black eyes that in anyone less likable than herself might be described as beady. Little escaped her, and her words were not to be disregarded. To be liked and trusted by her was a matter of pride. She held the household together at times when it could not have been easy.

And then Arthur. I was so attached to him that it is hard to be objective about him. Evelyn and Alec have both written of his love of cricket and of reading aloud and have sketched in the broad outline of his character, although their lines of approach have their differences. To me he was, as it were, both the Cheeryble brothers rolled into one and I could never have enough of the richness of tone and the enjoyment he so evidently felt in rolling out the line:

Beautiful Evelyn Hope is dead

or giving us a selection of Praed as he intoned to us from his armchair in the study. In spite of what I wrote as a schoolboy, Alec, when he was there, had with his neat correctness, his courtesy, which seemed animated by clockwork but which was none the less reassuring for that, a soothing effect on the house.

In the face of such imperturbable good nature, rows seemed unthinkable, and Evelyn put up resignedly with three-cornered talk about cricket and Middlesex's chances of winning the championship.

When the party was reduced to four, Arthur and Kate, Evelyn and myself, that is, things were different. Arthur loved telling stories, literary stories about Edmund Gosse, a relation of his, about Austin Dobson, about any number of authors, about publishing, about his firm's relations with Dickens, about anything that came into his head and I loved listening.

Evelyn emphatically did not. Sometimes he would content himself with sighing; sometimes he would say outright that he had heard the particular story his father was telling before—and not once but many times. Then it was the turn of Arthur to assume an air of meek martyrdom, an air calculated to bring out the worst in Evelyn, and the atmosphere round the dinner table would become sulphurous.

· · · · ·

Of course those words in the letter Arthur wrote to me, 'You do not despise the things that matter, or speak cynically of character', were an oblique, and not so oblique, reference to the growing, and from Arthur's point of view, disquieting, change that had come over Evelyn in his middle Oxford days. Alec was a model son; in Arthur's eyes, however tolerant, Evelyn was not.

And then there was the bottle of Emu Burgundy which, improbable though it may seem, had a positive effect on the course of Evelyn's career. Arthur considered that a glass of this brand of wine at dinner was good for him, and so, night after night, the squat, pot-bellied bottle stood on the table, an object Evelyn could not have loathed more had it contained some malignant and all-powerful djinn.

The word 'bourgeois' was not used much in those days, but that was what, to Evelyn, the Emu bottle was a symbol of, and he was determined to escape all that it stood for.

· · · · ·

Of course, when I stayed with Evelyn we were not always in the house. In *A Little Learning* he gives the impression that he explored London solely in the company of Alec's first wife. This was not so. We did a lot of exploring on our own, with him on the inside seat of the bus, and went to a lot of theatres together. Once he insisted that we should start from Underhill in the evening, spend the night wandering about London and walk back to Hampstead at dawn. I cannot remember why he was so keen on this but he was (he was a good deal keener than I was), and, when Evelyn was keen on anything, he generally got his way. Even when his sense of purpose and direction was erratic, as it was in some of his Oxford and immediate post-Oxford days, the thrust was there—he was like some nuclear-powered entity whizzing balefully about in space.

Anyway, down to London we walked. An hour or two was spent in the crypt of St Martin-in-the-Fields where the 'down-and-outs' of that time would shelter for the night. The purpose of this particular exercise is by no means clear for neither of us had a glimmering of social conscience and I am certain that Evelyn had not a thought of possible 'copy' in his mind. However, remarkably observant he was even if he did not appear to be. Anyway, we worked our way through Covent Garden and back up to Underhill in the dawn, as we had planned. A curious excursion which gave us a lot of satisfaction. The time of all this must have been the autumn of 1924, and it is odd that Evelyn and I were still on reasonably intimate terms considering that he was at Oxford and I was not. I had failed the history scholarship at Oriel and was not altogether sorry since I had the sense to know that Oxford, with the people I already knew there and others I would get to know, would be difficult with the amount of money I could rely on.

One of the reasons that we were still friends lay in the fact that, on the surface, I was doing a good deal better than Evelyn. In his book, for instance, Evelyn mentions the disproportionate pleasure given to him by the fact that Sir John Squire—J. C., 'Jack', Squire as he was then—accepted a wood-cut of his for *The London Mercury*. What he forgets to add is that it was I who got Jack to take it. I had been 'taken up' by the 'Squirearchy', which was then a powerful force in literary London, and a very pleasant experience it was. And then, in November 1924, I had my first novel published.

The novel was not a good one, but J. B. Priestley, who was then reading for the Bodley Head, thought it had enough promise to deserve publication; the reviews, though not the sales, vindicated him. The point is that when the Bodley Head made up its mind to go ahead and publish, I asked that Evelyn should be entrusted with the design of the dust-cover. Actually, Evelyn did two, both of them admirable—they are now at the University which has the letters. The Bodley Head, however, decided against them, and Evelyn behaved angelically. He did not, incidentally, think the novel was up to much, but that did not prevent him from being delighted for my sake—that gift of identifying himself with the affairs of his friends was still a marked feature of his nature.

Finally, I was acting as a kind of assistant editor on *The Guardian* (the old Church Weekly not the Manchester daily) under F. A. Iremonger.

There were in Iremonger, just as there were in Evelyn, traits of taste and character calculated to make the practice of Christianity difficult. Iremonger looked, and behaved, like a Colonel in one of the more expensive pre-1914 cavalry regiments. He liked the good, or, rather the best, things in life. He was a member of Boodles. Yet he lived for years in Bethnal Green and worked at Oxford House, which had its headquarters there. He was a disciplinarian, a perfectionist, an aristocrat, yet he forced his opinions to incline to the Left. He did not by nature suffer fools or, if it comes to that, people of moderate intelligence, gladly, yet he was always, or nearly always, a walking example of the more masculine, positive Christian virtues.

He wrote a model biography of William Temple,

whose intimate friend and honorary chaplain he was when Temple was at York, and, if the Primacy could be left in a will, there is little doubt whom Temple would have named as his successor. To have made him Archbishop of Canterbury would have been an inspired appointment, and Iremonger would have made a magnificent Archbishop, although he might, in that position, have proved rather too strong and positive a personality to suit Churchill. After being in charge of religious broadcasting at the B.B.C., they gave him the Deanery of Lichfield. I saw him again towards the end of his life. He was ill and frail at the time and, because of his ulcers, was living on boiled fish and milk, a diet which filled him with infinite distaste. Shortly afterwards he wrote to me from Lichfield to say that the only bearable thing about the place was the Deanery itself, and that he had given up to the Choir School. The two parts of that letter, the impatient intolerance, on the one hand, and the extent of the self-sacrifice, on the other, perfectly reflect the contrasting yet complementary strains in his nature.

There seem then to be parallels between the struggles that must have been inevitable in both himself and Evelyn (I do not think, incidentally, that he ever met Evelyn and, if he did, he would not have liked him) in pursuing a religion that preached meekness and humility. The fact that I worked for, and was befriended by, Iremonger was also of importance to me after the lamentable episode at the Ritz.

· · · · ·

The episode was hardly dramatic, indeed must have been invisible to anyone who might be watching and yet it altered—at the time it destroyed—the relationship between Evelyn and myself. On the afternoon I was to meet Evelyn and a mutual acquaintance (he was, as it happens, rich) for tea at the Ritz, I was not 'right' for the occasion. I forget what I was wearing but it was not appropriate and, to make things worse, I was, for some reason or other, carrying a cheap, cardboardish sort of dispatch-case. I did not feel like meeting Evelyn, above all, I did not feel like meeting him at the Ritz. I got there first and sat waiting feeling flustered and uncomfortable.

Evelyn knew it the moment he came in with our acquaintance, who, incidentally, was more Evelyn's friend than mine and was entirely innocent of doing anything more than, as it were, passively 'ganging up' with him in his attack on me. Evelyn knew it, and he went to work cruelly to do all he could to humiliate me. Of course, there was nothing violent or sensational about what happened; nothing happened at all except that Evelyn, in the most subtle and vindictive way known to him, went to work. I know that Evelyn always prided himself on his loyalty, even when he was well on in life, and I believe it did exist as far as some friends were concerned right up until the end, but I was never inclined to trust to it after that afternoon.

There was a streak of man-eating tiger in Evelyn, especially when what Cyril Connolly has called 'a certain coarseness of heart' had begun to take over, and on that afternoon at the Ritz it found expression because I had allowed my uneasiness to taint the air. Hitherto, in spite of our master–disciple, senior–junior, partnership, relation, I had proved adept enough at the game of exchanging insults, and had never feared Evelyn. That afternoon I had been afraid, and neither my nerve nor Evelyn's loyalty, to say nothing of that affection on which I had always counted, survived the test. It was a poor performance all round.

When I left the Ritz it seemed obvious that the friendship between Evelyn and myself was at an end.

It must now have been about the autumn of 1925 and

there had been signs for some time past that the links between us were loosening. It was inevitable. He had many friends, Terence Greenidge, for example, was one, and only one, of those who knew much more about him and his affairs at this time than I did. Besides, I wanted a different Evelyn, a reassuring, conforming Evelyn who would grow into the comfortable image of his father, and Evelyn, especially at that erratic and unpropitious period in his career, had no more intention of doing that than the then Prince of Wales had of becoming a replica of George V.

Besides, for some little time now I had been slowly pushed out on to the far periphery of Evelyn's interests. I was not asked, for instance, to take part in that film with Elsa Lanchester that so amused Evelyn and his Oxford circle at the time. It had been a marvellous privilege to have been a friend of the old Evelyn; to be a butt of the new would be unthinkable.

I might go to Underhill once or twice but it would probably be at the invitation of Arthur rather than of Evelyn. He was an acquaintance of my cousins, Joan and Francis Laking, and I might meet him there. We might find ourselves at, for instance, Gwen Otter's dinner table; we would certainly come across one another at one of the parties that were spreading like a not unamiable plague across the face of contemporary society. That would seem to be, that was, roughly the pattern of events and doubtless such tenuous connections would have dwindled to nothing if it had not been for two separate factors which from, roughly, the spring and early summer of 1927 to the spring and early summer of 1928 restored us to something like our old relationship. One was Olivia Plunket Greene; the other our respective marriages.

Olivia Plunket Greene has had a bad Press, a phrase that would have amused and puzzled her. There was Harold Acton, in his *Memoirs of an Aesthete*, who mentions her as possessing 'minute pursed lips and great goo-goo eyes' and, as Evelyn implies in *A Little Learning*, that was by no means adequate. Barbara Cartland, describing in *Follow My Leader* a game through Selfridges played by what the gossip columns of the day called 'the Bright Young People', wrote of her as having a 'dead-white expressionless face made up like a mask'. Alec wrote that she was 'a profound depressant', and with that judgement a part of her, if she could bring herself to be sufficiently interested, might well have agreed. C. M. Bowra obviously had her in his sights when he wrote of Evelyn's fatal habit of gravitating towards women who were of no possible use to him. Certainly it is difficult to think of Olivia as a person who would go about forwarding any man's career or, indeed, of pursuing any course of action with persistence, reason or consistency.

Evelyn was much in love with her and she, in her turn, was deeply attached to him. At the same time, that common sense which found so an incongruous a place in an eccentric, delicate and fundamentally unworldly personality, weighed and found wanting any question of marriage. Her affection for Evelyn was, then, precious to her but it worried her, and it was perception of this that led her to lower the barriers she normally kept erected against the world outside her family—to them, her mother Gwen, that is, and her two brothers, Richard and David, she was devoted.

I think I must have met her, probably through her brother Richard, about the spring of 1927 and she struck me at once as something rare and precious. She accepted my admiration, if only for the fact that she saw I understood the difficulties inherent in her relationship with Evelyn.

As for Evelyn, he, when he realised that Olivia trusted me, began once more to treat me in the old manner. The question of jealousy did not exist. My feeling for her was very different from Evelyn's, and there was nothing of strain or anxiety in it. That, indeed, was the thing that once more drew Evelyn to me for he could rely on my understanding of his emotions and on my appreciation of its object—many of his friends, I am sure, took Harold Acton's view of the 'minute pursed lips and great goo-goo eyes' and could not understand what he 'saw' in her. It annoyed him.

Everything connected with Olivia is apt to slide away from the rules and values of normal life, so that the bizarre becomes the commonplace. She had the unconscious knack of making the world seem *vulgar*—there is no other word for it—and therefore the desire to see her, to be assured that she did indeed inhabit the same earth as oneself, was strong. Sometimes it became irresistible, as Evelyn well knew, and as I had reason to believe myself. I was once writing on the Scarborough cricket festival for *The Times*, when everything suddenly seemed unbearable and I had to get in touch with Olivia. I left Yorkshire and the M.C.C. to their own devices, walked down to the post office and sent a telegram to Olivia which simply read 'Want to know if you are there.' She afterwards told me that she showed it to her mother and asked what on earth I meant. Gwen, with great good sense, replied that I wanted to know if she, Olivia, was still there, a palpable presence. She therefore wired back 'Am still here,' and I was content.

This communication between a Mayfair flat (if it was, at that moment, the Mayfair flat, for Olivia and Gwen seemed perpetually on the move) and the Press-box at Scarborough was a lunatic affair indeed, but it would have seemed as natural to Evelyn as it did to me. If I ever mentioned it to him there would have been no need for elaborate explanations of my motives, although *why* it was so important for me to hold a telegram from her in my hands, it is impossible to say.

But memories of Olivia tend to blend and yet to contradict. I suppose a montage of her would show the goo-goo eyes and Barbara Cartland's dead-white, masklike face; there would be a gramophone, a gin bottle and a cat in the foreground, while Brompton Oratory and the figure of a negro (it was the time of the Blackbirds, Paul Robeson—and Evelyn would not have been unaware of that formidable figure and his relationship with Olivia—and dear Florence Mills and Richard would give all-night parties at his house off Holland Park Avenue for them) would incongruously fill in the background. She was frequently the centre of uproar and outrage—she could, in fact, herself represent uproar and outrage—yet the quality that comes back most clearly across the years is her gift for sudden silence, a passive sort of stillness. Shaw makes his Archbishop say to St Joan that she was in love with religion, and I think Olivia was even in those days (she was then, in 1927, about 20) although I doubt whether either Evelyn or myself fully recognised the fact at the time. Finally, there was something not of this world about her, although she was nothing at all like, say, Barrie's Mary Rose.

How, then, would it be possible to be in love with a girl who was, at one and the same time, a ghost with a glass of gin in her hand, a *religieuse* and a Bright Young Person, sometimes wilful and silly? Then, of course, we all drank too much. I remember when I would go up to Oxford to see Evelyn during his early days there, his cry concerning alcohol was 'sustain the mood', but even Evelyn found that more difficult to do than to say. In those days he used to reproach me for my moderation; there was no need for him to do that any more.

Olivia, I think, drank because she was nervous of meeting people, which was odd because she was so entirely unconcerned about her own behaviour or what people 'thought' of it or her; she was as indifferent to all outward forms as she was to natural ambition or success. She was unconcerned or, indeed, ignorant of so much that went on. She would be quite capable, after dealing every day with the currency of the time, of suddenly and vehemently declaring that she had never seen a half-crown before, had no idea what it was or what it was supposed to do. That is not exactly a literal illustration of a disconcerting tendency of hers, but it is not far removed from one.

But then there was that other side of her that expressed itself in a silence and passivity that had a indescribable quality about them.

. . . . .

And so, through Olivia, Evelyn and I were once more on terms of friendliness, and this was to have momentous consequences for Evelyn. No one interested in Evelyn Waugh can possibly ignore the reality of her influence over him. The impression she made on him was deep, at a time when he himself was in deep waters.

Although Olivia had acted as an unconscious agent in restoring Evelyn and myself to something approximating our old relationship, it must not be supposed that at this time, the summer of 1927, say, that we saw a great deal of one another. Each of us had his own interests, his own circle of friends, of which the other knew little. It was a period when the graph of Evelyn's fortunes was turning ominously down. There was still an emotional turmoil going on within him with Olivia not primarily involved; outwardly, it was the near disastrous time of the Art School and the preposterous prep school.

Evelyn was taking a relish Byron would have appreciated in the wreck he seemed to be making of his life—the romanticism on which he fed in his early youth was not yet dead in him. Olivia would have fitted easily as a counter-balancing figure in a Byronic exercise in excessive self-disgust, such as Evelyn was capable of, although she would have been tart indeed in her expression of disapproval at so incongruous a role.

. . . . .

Still, more important for the immediate sequence of events, was the fact that Evelyn and I were once more in touch with one another. It was natural, therefore, in the new, or, rather, the old, order of things that I should hear one morning on the telephone that mock-gruff voice asking me how I dared write a tolerably good novel. This was my third and perhaps Evelyn was right—it was tolerably good, and it shared the fate of the others, admirable reviews and deplorable sales.

Anyway, there Evelyn and I were, on something like our old footing and meeting when geography and our respective interests allowed us. It was, at any rate, once more natural for me to be asked up to Underhill or to parties involving Evelyn in one way or another and natural for me to think of Evelyn in the same terms. At any rate I did give a small party at my Red Lion Square flat and I asked Evelyn and there he met the girl who was to become his first wife.

That girl was the Honourable Evelyn Gardner, and the courtesy title is spelt out in full, because it should be given its due weight in the curious equation which finally resolved itself in the marriage of the two sharply contrasting Evelyns. It is difficult without the aid of diaries to pin-point exact dates, but I think I introduced the two Evelyns to one another some time in the autumn of 1927.

I myself had known Evelyn Gardner for some little time before that, and here Call Boy's 1927 Derby helps to plot the time schedule. Evelyn Gardner and myself were fellow guests on a bus hired by the White Rajah of Sarawak for that particular Derby, and it was through the Sarawaks that I met her. She was a friend of—I think she was half engaged to—the Rajah's secretary, Barry Gifford, and somewhere or other I had met Barry Gifford and he introduced me to the Sarawak house in Portland Place. I went there fairly often, partly because the Ranee, a Brett and a vivacious personality with generous instincts, had an interest in the young and the 'arts', and partly because Noni, the eldest daughter then about 12, lovely in face and in mind, liked me.

There, at any rate, was Evelyn Gardner and a most pleasant, simple (the word here has its more attractive overtones) girl she was with a small up-turned nose and an engagingly ingenuous manner. A typical English miss? A typical English rose? Yes, perhaps. On the surface, certainly. She was sharing a flat at that time with Lady Pansy Pakenham over a tobacconist's shop off Sloane Square, and, when I got to know them better, I thought how lucky Evelyn was to have Pansy to 'look after' her. I don't suppose Pansy was more than a year or so older than Evelyn, but she was a person of such calm authority that it was natural to think of her in this 'looking after' capacity. She probably did no such thing, but there she was, as decorative as she was dependable, entirely, or so it seemed to me, certain of herself and where she was going—she was going, as it happened, to marry Henry Lamb, and there was no doubt as to the success of *that* marriage.

If I have given Pansy a 'governessy' image, then that image is grotesquely out of drawing—I think now that it was more Evelyn Gardner's apparent innocence, no, not exactly that so much as her seeming vulnerability, contrasted with Pansy's maturity, that gave this impression.

I think at that time that I underrated a certain strain

of toughness and sophistication in Evelyn Gardner, but that is by the way. At any rate, she was a girl it was impossible to dislike or, rather, I could imagine only one person who might dislike her, and that was Evelyn Waugh. One reason for this conviction was, I suppose, the fact that she was so completely unlike Olivia, although better psychology would have realised that the very contrast she made with Olivia, and all the things that exasperating girl stood for, might well have been an attraction.

And, again, there was that in Evelyn Waugh, at that period of his life at any rate, which itself was ready to respond to the simple and uncomplicated. There were, of course, sombre moods; there was the erratic restlessness of his mind; there was the strain inherent in his exaggerated social ambitions; there was the satire that was due soon to express itself on paper. But there was a side to him that rejoiced in the less exacting forms of humour. He was not a wit in the accepted sense of the word; rather he delighted in fantastic exaggeration, in acting out to the full his repertoire to burlesque ferocity, and he would roar with laughter at his own jokes. Evelyn Waugh could make a great deal of noise.

Perhaps the two Evelyns did not meet at my flat in Red Lion Square; it may have been that I asked the Ranee whether I could bring Evelyn Waugh along to Portland Place for a drink—Evelyn was, of course, then unknown outside his particular circle at Oxford and was not sought out by hostesses. If he did come first to Portland Place, I do not think he went there again, for, with the two Evelyns being at once attracted to one another, there was poor Barry Gifford left posing a problem of some embarrassment.

Whether at Portland Place or Red Lion Square, however, the meeting took place and the consequences were startling. The time, then, was somewhere in the autumn–

winter of 1927 and, some weeks afterwards, I myself underwent something of the same experience as that which befell the two Evelyns—falling in love at first sight, that is. I went to a dance somewhere, saw an exquisite golden girl, danced with her for hours, fell madly in love and then, at about 3.30, realised that I had to change out of evening dress and catch a train to Huddersfield to report for *The Times* on that town's cup-tie with West Ham United—I still remember that particular match. Just before I left, I lost sight of the girl and realised in a panic that I did not know who she was, who her parents were or where she lived—all I knew was her name was Anthea Gamble. Luckily Roger Fulford was still at the dance and he told me that she was the daughter of the Dean of Exeter.

That was good enough for me and from the George Hotel, Huddersfield, that cup-tie Saturday evening, with cloth caps and broad Yorkshire accents all round me, I wrote to Anthea proposing marriage. I was accepted, went down the next week to Exeter and was approved of by Maud Gamble, Anthea's mother. The only difficulty was that the Dean was in London, but lunch was fixed with him at the Athenaeum and I got over that hurdle too. I think I know why now, but at the time it seemed strange, for I was far from being an eligible *parti*. True, I was writing for *The Times* and that, in those days, did indeed carry distinction, but I was not yet a member of the editorial staff, and *The Times* then believed that payment was a kind of pocket money to men who, since they were on *The Times*, automatically must have private money of their own. True again, I had three novels to my credit—it was a stroke of luck that Maud Gamble had read the third which Evelyn had accusingly stated was tolerably good—but my 'success' in that field remained obstinately one *d'estime*, and refused to budge out of that bracket. Anthea, on the other hand, was beautiful and intelligent enough to have the pick of the West Country, let alone of Devonshire.

My whole whirlwind affair with Anthea, culminating in my engagement, had an air of unreality about it. Evelyn was in a similar position to my own, and, at this particular moment, he had even less to offer Evelyn Gardner than I had to offer Anthea, although of course his circumstances were to undergo a dramatic change soon after this marriage with the instant success of *Decline and Fall*.

. . . . .

And so Evelyn and I were proceeding by roughly parallel paths towards our respective marriages.

I remember once that I was alone with Pansy in her Sloane Square flat and I said that, of our three approaching marriages, I was certain that hers with Henry Lamb would be a success. I thought mine had a 50–50 chance (the coin was destined, in tragic circumstances, to fall against me) while I was convinced that that of the two Evelyns would fail. I do not think she went so far as to disagree.

And so to perhaps the most precious of all my memories concerning Evelyn. The time must have been early in January 1928—Evelyn, I think, was to go back to that prep school for the spring term. At any rate I was staying the night at Underhill, and, after Arthur and Kate had gone to bed, he told me he had something to show, or, rather to read, to me. He had already finished his *Rossetti* (I have a presentation copy dated April 19, 1928, but whether that was the actual publication day or not I would not like to say) but he had not any great hopes that it would make him famous overnight.

What he in fact read to me that night, sitting in the chair where Arthur was wont to proclaim that beautiful

Evelyn Hope was dead, were the first fifty or so pages of *Decline and Fall*. A happiness, a hilarity, sustained him that night, and I was back giving him my unstinted admiration as I did at Lancing. It was marvellously funny and he knew that it was. As was his habit in those old, innocent days, he roared with laughter at his own comic invention.

But there was a serious side to Evelyn's attitude toward the book. It was quite time Evelyn produced something to prove to the world that he was the remarkable person his friends knew him to be. It was unthinkable, especially in view of his forthcoming marriage, that he should go on teaching at third-rate schools; neither had his time in London at the Art School been a fruitful one.

He knew, as I did, that he had a winner in *Decline and Fall*, but when he had finished reading, doubt intruded. All would be well once it was published, but *would* it ever be published? He foresaw difficulties with publishers who were fearful in those days of anything 'daring', let alone comedy which could be construed as indecent. He was justified in his fears—Duckworth, who were bringing out his *Rossetti*, refused to handle it. There was always Chapman and Hall, of course, but I remember Evelyn on that night saying that he knew Arthur would not like it and that he was reluctant to saddle his father with what was bound to be to him, Arthur, that is, a painful choice.

And so we had enough to be serious about. Evelyn was in the position of a man who had drawn a winning sweepstake ticket but had forgotten where he put it and so is not certain whether he will ever be able to cash it. There in his hands was a marvellously original piece of comic writing—it goes off towards the end but the first three-quarters are superb—but would anyone ever be able to read it? I doubt whether either of us quite visualised the extent of the success it was to achieve, but that it would give him a reputation and launch him, as it were, on a career after a perilous period of drifting, seemed clear.

But supposing it was not destined to, suppose the difficulties of censorship proved too much or publishers too obtuse, what then would have been Evelyn's future?

It might well have been dark indeed for Evelyn always showed a reckless inclination to go to extremes, to involve himself totally in his immediate preoccupations. What is more, he was, for one of his acute intelligence and formidable brain, surprisingly lacking in the compass directions provided by theory and thought. He loved the excesses of absurdity; to him people perpetually were playing parts in some wild extravaganza of his own imagining—anybody less of an intellectual I have seldom met. Thus although his own ideas on the manner and practice of writing clearly were formed, he seldom engaged in long and abstract discussion concerning these or anyone else's books, pictures etc., although his reading and the critical, iconoclastic bent of his mind enabled him to do so whenever he was with those he trusted—or, of course, on paper. He was capable of shrewd snap judgements and, in public at least, that was that. In our playgoing days, he 'liked' *R.U.R.*, for instance, and 'disliked' *Abraham Lincoln*: the criticism, especially when older people were about, rarely rose above that level. Evelyn was capable of thinking things out all right—his *Rossetti*, after all, contained some pretty solid material—only it was part of his personality, and of one of the disguises that went with it, to express himself in unremarkable and elementary terms. With his inner life it was very different, and I always was curious as to why the practice of writing in illuminated script had such a fascination for him. Perhaps one reason was that it was so totally divorced from the pressures and frictions of normal existence; certainly it fitted in with the *fin-de-siècle* romanticism that still exercised a certain influence over him.

But this tendency, especially in the company of comparative strangers, to confine himself to platitudes went back to the earlier days of our friendship and to the time Evelyn was still in his teens. I remember that in those days the Waughs would give a kind of combination of an 'At Home' and a cocktail party at which people like St John Ervine, so prickly and contentious in print, so kindly in conversation, G. B. Stern, Sylvia Gosse, the booming Bourchier Evelyn has so admirably described in *A Little Learning*, and many others, would gather and then it was Evelyn's custom to sink himself into the background and to become, to all intents and purposes, anonymous.

A. D. Peters, a life-long friend of Alec Waugh's and of the Waugh family who read this book in MS., remarked that he had no idea that Evelyn as an 18-year-old was in any way outstanding. His memory of him when he used to meet him at Underhill is that of a silent listener to the conversation, and certainly this instinct of his to, as it were, disappear from sight when there were other people about was marked. Anything, from their point of view, less like a young genius bubbling over with iridescent ideas and coruscating epigrams it would be impossible to conceive, yet all the while Evelyn was inwardly forming the people about him into preposterous, farcical shapes and placing them in those incongruous juxtapositions that so delighted him.

Again, he disliked music and the ballet, and yet we would find ourselves walking quietly, as though in homage, when we passed Pavlova's home in Hampstead.

But when Diaghilev and his Russian ballet appeared on the scene we were both of us bowled over. Once again. however, I don't think it ever occurred to Evelyn to analyse the reason. He might mention the excitement of the violent clash of colour and of movement, but I don't think that he went further. The days of his absurd enthusiasm for James Branch Cabell were, of course, in the past and I remember him insisting that I buy *The Wasteland*. He saw the outstanding merits of the poem; he did not, as I remember, see it as a landmark in the literary evolution of the time.

His reactions were still subjective and instinctive and he was at all times extreme in his response to his friends and the ideas they represented—or he fancied they represented. He remarks very truly in *A Little Learning* that he fell in love with the whole family of Plunket Greenes—just as he 'fell in hate', as it were, with poor Crutwell at Oxford—and it was precisely this fervour (although it was well enough disguised on the surface), this lack of proportion, that so disturbed Olivia although she herself disliked all that was temperate. He wanted to immerse himself in whatever it was that held his interest at the time, to become involved. He was always a person of action, one who delighted in the uncomplicated challenge it afforded. A little time before this an incident occurred which illustrated this side of his nature.

We had found ourselves at a party given by two artists, one, I believe, admirable, who were rather older than we were. I had heard them called 'pansies' and, although my continuing ignorance on this subject prevented me from understanding precisely what the word meant, I disliked it and its implications. I had had enough to drink that evening to declare that my hosts and, as far as I could guess, the majority of his guests, fell into the pansy category, and that therefore I found them distasteful.

The elder of the two artists behaved perfectly. He told me I did not know what I was talking about, that I had been guilty of disgraceful discourtesy and asked me to leave the house. Some of his guests, however, seemed disinclined for the matter to be resolved in so civilised a way. They thought I should be taught a lesson—and a painful one. It was at this moment, when ringed round with a circle of menacing young men, that I caught sight of Evelyn at the far end of the studio. '*À moi*, Evelyn!' I called out with the theatricality of the tipsy, '*à moi*', and at once he came charging down the long room like a rugger forward with the line in sight. He did not know what the quarrel was about and cared less. It was less a question of standing by me than getting involved in physical action—and that he revelled in. For a moment or two there was a real prospect of a stand-up fight with the odds heavily against us, but somehow or other the first blow was never struck and we found ourselves out in the street with the door closed behind us.

I was sober enough immediately to be remorseful both at my own conduct and at having cut short the party for Evelyn. He did not see it at all that way, and if he had any regrets, it was for the fact that he had been cheated out of a fight.

Direct action was what appealed to Evelyn, and this was never more obvious than in his relationship with alcohol. That evening while we were talking about the possibility of *Decline and Fall* never being published, I remember thinking that rejection of it might, from this particular point of view, be especially catastrophic. He could not go on declining into obscurity and failure; indeed he went so far as to attempt suicide, an effort foiled in the best Evelyn Waugh tradition by a swarm of jellyfish. This, of course, he recounts in *A Little Learning*; I knew nothing about it and I don't think anybody else did either.

What I was contemplating that evening was the possibility of a more prolonged form of suicide through drink. We all at that time drank too much, but it was generally through unthinking weakness, a desire to get the party going and to keep it that way, or because it was the thing to do, the line of least resistance.

It was not at all that way with Evelyn. He went at the

bottle as though he was engaged in a desperate, murderous struggle with one who was at the same time deadly enemy and devoted comrade. It was almost a combat on a physical level, Evelyn's own favourite field, with seconds out.

I remember a curious and disquieting incident in connection with this. For some reason or other Audrey Lucas, the daughter of 'E. V.' who was one of Arthur's most intimate friends, and I were to meet Evelyn at lunch time at a little pub near the British Museum. When we got there Evelyn was on the verge of passing out into unconsciousness, but what I remember even more than his swaying figure, a boxer who is still on his feet but who has received a knock-out blow, was the awed expression of the landlord who looked fearfully at him and told us again and again that he had 'never seen anything like it'.

We were too preoccupied with the task of finding a taxi and getting Evelyn into it to worry about asking him what he meant, but I suppose Evelyn had not been waiting for us for more than twenty minutes or so and that what so impressed the landlord, who must have had considerable experience of such matters, was the way Evelyn had so ferociously gone about the task of drinking himself insensible.

The phrase 'hitting the bottle' has a peculiar aptness here, but it tells only half the story, for Evelyn very well knew that the bottle could hit back at him. There they were in the ring, two redoubtable opponents and friends, asking and giving no quarter. What the landlord had witnessed in fact was a kind of boxing bout with the two principals going at it hammer-and-tongs from the start.

Evelyn's drinking at that time was not, then, the sort of part-time vice in which most of us indulged; it was a serious, not to say a deadly business, and it was this aspect of affairs which was so disturbing to contemplate should

Decline and Fall fail to find a publisher or if it did, if it were to meet with the tepid kind of reception that greeted his *Rossetti*.

Evelyn needed success at that time and he needed it badly and by no means solely for the normal material reasons, although they naturally came into it. It was clear that evening that Evelyn's whole future was in the balance, and that the brilliance of what he had read would make it harder for him to bear if fate tilted things the wrong way.

Fate did not, although success, as it happened, was destined to provide Evelyn with almost as many problems as failure would have done, but then at that particular stage in his life he was at his most dangerous and unpredictable. Perhaps there was nothing that could have provided him with content and put him on an even keel, but then contentment and even keels are not particularly desirable things in the eyes of the young, especially if they are charged with an excess of talent and vitality.

On the credit side in Evelyn's immediate future was the fact that *Vile Bodies* was destined to be an even greater success than *Decline and Fall*. On the debit, the collapse of his marriage. I have never been able to convince myself that this disaster—for disaster, of course, it must have been—had such traumatic consequences for Evelyn as those who knew him afterwards seem inclined to believe, but then that was, perhaps, because the two Evelyns had always appeared to me so unsuited to one another that I could never believe in the possibility of a life-long union between them.

There was also the fact that I have already touched on, the fact that about both our marriages there was an air of what might be called glamorous unreality. Also, although we were both in our twenty-fifth year, we were too young, too unprepared, for marriage. This reference to age may seem fantastic to those who think nothing of marrying at seventeen, but then the whole trend of our upbringing inclined us away from thoughts of domesticity and the bringing up of children—in many ways we were overgrown children ourselves, and at the back of our minds I think we recognised it.

Finally, and most important, there was Evelyn's coming conversion to Roman Catholicism which was, of course, profoundly to affect him in ways of which I knew nothing and at which I could not guess. Certainly it never occurred to me as even the remotest of the many possibilities that crossed my mind as we stayed up talking that night.

. . . . .

There is one final incident. At the end of our honeymoon Anthea and I came back to London and stayed a few nights at Underhill. When we got down to breakfast the first morning—it must have been rather late for Arthur had gone off to Chapman and Hall—there was Evelyn sitting at a writing desk that was n ia kind of recess in the dining room. He was writing away with intense concentration and that he was angry was obvious from the back of his neck.

We asked him what was the matter and it appeared that he was writing a letter of protest to the Editor of *The Times Literary Supplement*, since that paper had published a review of his *Rossetti*, tucked away in small print among the 'Books Received' pages, in which the author was referred to as 'Miss Waugh'. This infuriated him, but it struck us as funny since anything more unlike a 'Miss Waugh' than the formidable young man, aggressive in manner and built on the lines of a light-weight fighting bull, it would be impossible to imagine.

Evelyn, however, was not to be mollified. Part of the reason for his very real annoyance lay, I think, in the fact that the effect of much of his humour sprang from a rigidly literal interpretation of what was not meant to be literally interpreted. Take the character in *Vile Bodies* who, because she wears an armlet proclaiming her to be a 'Spare Driver', insists on acting precisely as that when the emergency arises; take the case of the split polo sticks in *Scoop. The Times Literary Supplement* had called him 'Miss Waugh' and therefore the absurd misapprehension meant more to him than it would to someone with a mind less acutely concerned with such matters.

There is not to be here any impersonal criticism of Evelyn as a writer, but I think that this business of literal, dead-pan interpretation as the mainspring of his comic invention has been overlooked. It was a pose, a gambit, rather, that he carried into normal life as well. It was not only correctitude in clothes that he insisted on; a clipped, concise formality of manner was an admirable disguise for that streak of outrageous anarchism that ran deep in him. His rudeness, too, was the more effective for appearing as part of a kind of minuet of manners. In the end it all came down to a question of style—and Evelyn was always a stylist.

That 'Miss Waugh' business rankled, and, although after a time, he was willing to laugh at it, it was, as it were, dutiful laughter without humour or appreciation. He did not forgive, or forget, certain things easily, and this was one of them. Besides, the *Rossetti* book was a failure.

There is little else to tell. His marriage followed in a few weeks and then *Decline and Fall* achieved its immediate success. Money worries which had plagued Evelyn since his early days at Oxford, were, by a miracle, although one in which he believed as he had shown at that reading at Underhill, removed, and the world was open to him.

Rumours that all was not going well with the marriage

began to drift about shortly after the Evelyns moved into that Canonbury Square flat, and here our experiences, as they had before our weddings, shared similarities. At any rate some time in the late summer of 1930 I found that I had no more use for my flat in Oakley Street than Evelyn had for his Canonbury one. And so I moved into it and there I stayed until April 2, 1931, when a decisive, though temporary, event in my life rendered that flat, in its turn, superfluous. I moved out, although whether I saw Evelyn about the arrangements for winding up the lease, handing over the keys and all the rest of it or whether it was done through an agent I cannot remember. If I did see Evelyn then it was at any rate the last time I saw him to speak to. I did see him, however, once more.

Epilogue

The time was about the end of the war, and Evelyn was walking down Whitehall. He had aged very little at first, superficial sight, but his square, strong body had grown thicker and his face was set in heavy, self-absorbed lines of menace and of sadness. It would be wrong to suggest that his carved look represented a permanent state of mind, but there it was as he walked down Whitehall deep in his own thoughts and oblivious of the people round him.

An impulse to go up to him was checked as soon as it was formed. Had the occasion been 10 years later when I was happy and confident in my second marriage, things might have been different. It needed confidence to tackle Evelyn and confidence was, at that moment, lacking. If the old gambit of 'Oh, Evelyn, that face!' had been tried, there was little likelihood that it would have succeeded. Evelyn had gone very far since those days, although there remains a doubt as to whether that gloriously optimistic prophecy 'You'll be greater because you are a creator' was as fulfilled as, by any ordinary count, it appears to have been.

But then Evelyn was no ordinary person and is not to be judged by ordinary standards. Considering his mastery of English prose, his achievements should have been even greater than they were. And there remains that baffling mystery, *The Ordeal of Gilbert Pinfold.* Why should Evelyn, who publicly and ostentatiously paraded his right to privacy, so extravagantly scatter clues to his own personality in what was, after all, supposed to be a novel—even allowing for the fact that all his novels contained an element of autobiography? Why turn it into a kind of paperchase leading to the very heart of his identity? But then if Evelyn did not do the kind of things he did, he would not have been the writer he was.

If *Gilbert Pinfold* was a kind of exercise in self-revelation and laceration, with its unbearable cry of 'Why does everybody except me find it so easy to be nice?,' *A Little Learning* hit out at others. It is not necessary to discuss it in any detail, although it achieves the fascination of being the worst book Evelyn ever wrote. In it he was concerned with closing doors, and since I was associated both with a public school that failed him by not being Eton, with the bottle of Emu Burgundy, with Arthur Waugh and with Underhill, it was inevitable that I should be eradicated from his life as he put the record on paper. Moreover I always have had the feeling that, since I introduced him to his first wife, he subconsciously associated me with, and blamed me for, the failure of a marriage that afterward he would never allow to be mentioned—the extracts, or, rather, the lack of them, in the Diaries are significant here.

But *A Fragment of Friendship* is the title of this book and a fragment of friendship it was. It may be inconsiderable in size and it broke off to leave jagged edges, but some of its facets glow with a brilliance that came from the magic of Evelyn's personality and it will always remain precious. 'The marvellous boy'—the phrase will not be banished.

What a fantastically inspiring companion he could be, and, although it was often banished to cobwebby corners by its imperious master, there was always a generous spirit lurking somewhere behind that aggressive, even murderous, exterior.

The full contents of the letter Evelyn wrote in reply

to my own about *A Little Learning* dated September 9, 1964, are not for publication. I may, however, reproduce the last words: '. . . forgive me in the name of our old friendship . . . Yours ever affectionately, Evelyn.' The shout up the valley of 'Weak tea and cold buttered toast, my God!' rings in my ears as I echo those final words: 'Yours ever affectionately . . .'

There is little to add, except perhaps to wonder whether I have not made Evelyn too much a reflection of personal predilection. Perhaps he (and Olivia, for that matter) were always outrageous, rogues, whatever their outward appearance, who never belonged to any tame, domestic herd.

Perhaps Evelyn had never been at home in the tranquil harbour of Underhill but had always been in spirit one with the pirate captain he was to become, driving his carven ship through frantic seas of alcohol, torn and tossed by the storms of his own temperament, flying colours with high armorial devices which were indeed open to challenge, but which would be defended to the last breath of a soul dedicated to the extremes of its own concept of fidelity.

A lunatic captain then, firing broadsides into the elements that raged round him, aiming often, with maniac precision of eye, at some innocent vessel going primly about its lawful occasions, or at some old ship of his acquaintance which had once accompanied him on a stage of his dangerous and unpredictable voyage. There was to be no port after stormy seas for such a captain and such a treasure ship as he commanded, and no land to be sighted, although perhaps the ghostly echo of a cathedral bell would sound through the mists that hedged him in and blinded his eyes. Still, he saw visions enough, although the record of them as he put them down in disciplined, ordered prose was at odds with their inward anarchy and despair.

At least a great talent, genius perhaps, was at work there, and interpretations of the human being in whom it was housed, interpretations made more difficult by the eccentric chart to its secrets he himself provided, will go on as long as the books are read. About the books there is certainty; about their author, perpetual, contradictory speculation.

That is the end. There is no more.